PETER BLAND

SELECTED POEMS

CARCANET

for Karen, Joanna, and Carl

First published in 1998 by
Carcanet Press Limited
4th Floor, Conavon Court
12-16 Blackfriars Street
Manchester M3 5BQ

A CIP catalogue record for this book
is available from the British Library
ISBN 1 85754 357 2

The publisher acknowledges financial assistance
from the Arts Council of England

Set in 10pt Horley Old Style by Bryan Williamson, Frome
Printed and bound in England by SRP Ltd, Exeter

Contents

Acknowledgements

Most of the poems in this selection have been previously published in *My Side of the Story* (Mate Books, Auckland, 1964), *The Man with the Carpet Bag* (Caxton Press, Christchurch, 1972), *Mr Maui, Stone Tents*, and *The Crusoe Factor* (London Magazine Editions, 1976, 1981, 1985), *Selected Poems* (John McIndoe, Dunedin, 1986) and *Paper Boats* (John McIndoe, Dunedin, 1991). A number of poems from *My Side of the Story* and *Stone Tents* were also published by Wai-Te-Ata Press, Victoria University, Wellington, in two booklets entitled *Domestic Interiors* (1964) and *Primitives* (1979).

Individual poems have been published in *Sport, Quote/Unquote, The New Zealand Listener, Landfall, Islands, Mate, Metro, Poetry Australia, London Magazine, The Honest Ulsterman, The Observer, Times Literary Supplement, PN Review, Printout* and *The Independent*.

The poem 'A Last Note from Menton' was the runner-up in the 1990 *Observer*/Arvon Foundation International Poetry Competition.

The author gratefully acknowledges assistance from the Queen Elizabeth II Arts Council of New Zealand during the writing of *Embarkations*.

1

The Old Country

Lament for a Lost Generation

Between V-J Day and 1951
we wore our first grey longs.
Drab, insular, short of vitamin C,
much given to fags and the fumbled grope

we became – like prefabs
or the last steam train –
something slightly embarrassing
that goes on and on: fodder for talks like

The Ration-Book Age or
The Wartime Growth of the Working Mum.
We were few; conceived in the slump;
brought up in shelters and under the stairs;

eleven-plus boys; post-war conscripts
who lowered the flag on better days.
What we lacked was a style!
We were make-do-and-menders,

utility-grey men, the last of a line.
You can tell us a mile off, even now;
there's a touch of austerity
under the eyes; a hint of carbolic

in our after-shave; a lasting doubt
about the next good time.

Two Family Snaps

1 *In a Council-House Backyard (Circa 1925)*

Here's Mum modelling her Susan Lenglen gear
with the penny-a-week insurance man
looking amazed at this ripe
housewife in white silk stockings leaning
over the clothesline. Over

the fence the neighbours' kids
mime her poses. They wink and strut
waving their Great Exhibition mugs. Mum
was much admired by a neighbourhood
that knew a bit of class when they saw it.

Talent will out, they all said.
It never did, but the neighbours
still applauded – being more
than faithful to those of their own
who always made the most of their lot.

2 *Big Game (Circa 1928)*

Here's Dad in Africa living it up
with a dead pig under his foot.
He's got a big cigar and an even bigger gun.
All around him there's space
and hordes of black naked lasses.

Just the place for a Bradford lad
brought up on Wesley and smog.
No wonder he's enjoying himself,
killing and screwing and making a profit.
When this was taken he was nearly forty.

Another few months and they shipped him home
to work on the ledgers. He packed life up
but took another twenty years to drop off.
I'm looking at an Empire in its heyday.
Even the dead pig is laughing.

Sunday School – 1945

Christ was nice, dressed in white,
being kind to donkeys and kids:
but you knew he was going to get it once
he'd whipped the money-men. No one
messed with that lot and lived!

It was his Dad I didn't trust . . .
not old Joseph but the one who yelled
out of a cloud or a bush. He
was rough, always shaking his fist
and looking for Philistines to kill.

With a Dad like that it must have been tough
to go back home, to leave Peter and John
and the rest of that gang with whom he'd come
to love this world, walking its fields,
sharing their wine and bread.

Regression

Bring me my fags and my flat cap
it's that Fifties feeling – like smog in the streets.
In prime rose-gardens the upper classes
are dispensing charity. God
is boss of the Sunday-School treat.

Brmmm . . . Brmmm . . . a workers' bus has just
parked inside my head. It's full
of turbaned Mums, drowned sailors, fatherless kids.
(There's a war on or one's just gone or one's
next on the list.) On factory estates

coffins are going in and out in shifts.
Thank god we're off! This bus won't stop
till it gets to Heaven via Scarborough sands.
Bring me my favourite Sunday-School print
of gentle Jesus on a donkey's back. Where

did he get that tan? And those palms
only grow indoors at *The Grand*. When our
bus gets stuck (more oil on those sands)
the Mums put up curtains and call it 'home'.
Grey riderless donkeys go galloping past.

A Liverpool Council-House – 1940

'*Show us the African room, yes, the African room . . .*'
a museum for Dad's depression years:
a working-class lad on the Ivory Coast.

Ten years retired his small front room
was still an Aladdin's cave for those
brought up on cabbages and rose-hip juice.

'*Show us the African room,*' we begged
and banged on that door kept locked for guests
who never arrived, even after the war,

having gone to their graves or to higher things
in government offices. Dad kept snaps
of dignitaries he'd met; mad Muslim chiefs;

Governors in cricket slacks; dark women
grinning – all breasts and teeth.
Inside the African room time ceased . . .

Stools were elephants' feet, vases bloomed
with spears and arrows. Kids queued up
to peep through the keyhole at a living tomb
where father ruled and the sun never set.

Jungle Smoke – Liverpool 1942

Two deck-chairs stamped SS NIGERIA
were the best Mum could manage
for our small front room. I'd
have settled for something more solid
like the twelve-foot settee some refugees
rescued from a bombed-out Odeon and installed
in the council-house next door. Mum
declared that our chairs were 'from better days'
when father travelled and Britannia ruled
pretty well everything south of Liverpool.
Dad sucked his pipe till it blackened the walls.
'Jungle smoke,' Mum called it, watching him cut
his tobacco straight from the plug. Marooned
with his wireless and gas-mask, Dad
waited 'for the end'. Of what? The war

I'd supposed . . . but, looking back,
more likely he sensed the end of an age
when horizons were infinite and rivers pushed
remorselessly inland. Night
after night he puffed out smoke
like a stranded steamer with an oily stack
while, hung above maps of the Russian front,
a Pears' print of *Bubbles* stared soulfully back.

Meringues

Meringues at Rowntrees (Scarborough '44);
a paino trio; views of the bay;
waitresses dressed like maids.
Through medallion windows
toy ships are sailing. It's hot.
The potted palms have fainted.

Mother's arms are lemony and sweet.
She's wearing her floppy hat
and that Myrna Loy smile
that brings men running.
They buy me pop and send me off
to gawp at the trawler-boats.

Up close they're dirty and grey
(not like the postcards of them
with sunset sails)
and the men who work them
are hungry-looking. They gob a lot
and don't talk cricket.

Back home Mum arrives at our council-house
in a chauffeured Rolls
(but I'm a trawlerman
I grunt and say nothing).
Holiday girls ignore us
and we know it.

Recollections of a Ministry of Munitions Housing Estate – 1944

Fifteen in our street dead of cancer
from TNT – death's pollen on the lungs.
That was '44, an Indian summer:
we gorged on home-made blackberry jam.

The factory pumped out bombs –
five-hundred pounders . . . 'To Adolph
from Tom and Alice.' Hamburg vanished
along with lots of Alices and Toms.

Slowly Mother's skin turned yellow.
You couldn't scrub it off.
She shone as bright as our pet canary
who sang when they switched the searchlights on.

Northern Funerals – 1942

We'd travel silently over the moors
in a long cortège of black Wolseleys owned
by uncles in local government. It was cold.
We clutched hot-water bottles in knitted covers
(summer cottages with roses round the door).
'Home', that night, was where we ate supper
after burying the host. Even
in wartime there was a funeral roast
(mostly 'obtained' by a good-looking aunt
from a Yank in company stores). Being
well-fed and 'as warm as toast'
was a state of grace to set against
each grave where the neighbours came to talk . . .
That lad doesn't give a damn! Not true,
but tears always froze on those cold moors
before the heart could squeeze them out. Death
made himself known as we turned to go. He sat
next to me when they slammed the car door,
one of the family, daring me to look up,
clutching his hottie all the way home.

The Parental Bedroom

A tomb or chapel smell about it. Always
so largely quiet – something unforgiven
about such silence. Looking in
at that huge slab of smoothed-down linen,
the bedside gadgets, rows of pills, the thin
smooth silky stuff that crammed out cupboards,
I sensed some house-worn secret hidden
beneath the camphored holiness. So

often when guarding my parents' absence
I'd dare that toe-deep silence, creep
consciously alone along the landing,
enter sidewise like a crab; within,
grab at the tattered *Mastery of Sex*,
drink brandy from a glass empty of teeth,
and breathe my medicinal breath in mirrors;
my blood loud as a clock; my feet

cold as the plastic gadgets I could finger
but never quite believe. Those mirrors,
those blood-loud clocks and thieving fingers
chasing me to the shed downstairs
where, page by page, I'd probe by heart
that guide-book to Love's working parts.
They must have guessed, yet never barred the way
between their chapel and my hermit's cave.

Art Deco

A Thirties idyll, something bright and cheerful
to jazz up damp distempered walls. . . .
I remember best a metal yacht on the mantle
safely sailing through poverty and war.
Won at a whist-drive it was stamped 'Pure Silver'
but turned out to be nickel-plated chrome.

Our 40 watt bulb, darkly shaded,
gave its deck a delicate rosy glow.
'Tahitian red,' mum said, always naming
places she would feel at home.
One by one – mum, dad, sailor brothers –
the family slipped quietly overboard.

When it berthed at the salerooms in '49
that gleaming con-job had outsailed them all.

London – 1953

A bag of biscuits lasts three days.
I keep the ledgers from S to U
in a white shirt on a Dickens stool.
Eight hours of copperplate. My fingers
are permanently blue. The girls

in the caféteria look middle-aged.
They listen, all day, to Johnnie Ray
singing 'Cry' on pirate radio. I
sleep in a basement off Dorset Place
with a visiting communist from Wales.

On Sundays we visit Marx's tomb.
I envy Marx his family room
where wives and children gave him space
to re-invent the rules. It's
a city of émigrés but a village still

for the loud indigenous rich. I've bought
my smog-mask (half-a-week's wage)
and some Brighton rock going cheap (it's
dated '52). My finer thoughts
keep me pure but caged. I'm in love

with a princess from *Swan Lake*
but can't believe ballet girls ever screw.
In a wonderfully swampy week of wet dreams
Carmen Miranda feeds me grapes. Lust
is technicolour in a year of gloom.

My communist friend is walking back to Wales.

Voyages

Saturday morning at the Scarborough *Odeon*
and trawlers in harbour
hooting through fog
are heard above Laughton on *The Bounty*
roaring his wig off. *U-boats*

shell the beach. For a week
the tide is littered with arms and legs.
In a Peasholm park paddle-boat
kids play pirates. Horizons
are endless. *'Come in No 1!'*

A chill February morning out of Glasgow;
an immigrant ship, full of surplus flesh,
limps in Cook's wake towards the Pacific . . .
Light scalds. Space sinks in.
Personal history flakes like burnt skin.

2

New Zealand
1958-1966

Wellington

A city of cenotaphs and tram-car sonnets . . .
Broad-breasted town, thy swarded mounds
More numerous than Rome's . . . We hang
Our houses out like washing to a breeze
That warns us of Scott's death-wish in the south.

The last colonial outpost . . . Perhaps
The liveliest capital since the Vatican.
Arriving, anchored where Victoria's brigs
Banged bibles and brass cannon, I'd
Marvelled at hotels like pink casinos,

Wharves like sea-side cafés, terraced hills
Of rainbow-bright façades and cubist houses.
The gentleman's convenience in mid-town
I'd taken for a temple, and the people
Splashing in Oriental Bay seemed crowds

Of sun-gods spilt from a Picasso painting.
Let's blame it on the light! I stand
Committed to imaginary landfalls . . .
The back door of a British council house
Could only lead out to the new Jerusalem:
Blake's burning bow was bound to scorch my hand.

Hills, Hutt Valley

Not fierce, mysterious, or inviting even
But, like the suburbs they surround,
Monotonous and easy to get lost in:
The lower slopes a useful place for tips.

Bulldozed for new roads or to clear the slips
That rain impermanence, they show
A bare back scratched with gorse. At night
They grow into the dark and are at home.

Only when the wandering eye is fresh
To everyday acceptance, do they flow
Into more than mere evergreen. Back from the road
They breathe a damp virginity that craves

Invasion of a sort. Stray hunters know
That paradox of bareness and profusion
Where the randy stag and sterile rifle cough
Like man and wife locked in a brooding room.

Kumara God

Three days and still the slow fogged rain
drifts inland. All across the valley
light melts to clusters of steamed-up panes.
All's formlessness. A sharpened will
won't chip us free of it. It's
a melting back, an elemental drift
beyond time or season . . .

                      And so I bring
the little stone cramped kumara god
in from the garden, take down the clock
and leave him there, upon the mantlepiece,
to be my curled-in self, grown
old in embryo, slightly sardonic . . .
feeling around me this slow retreat
of lives gone underground, of sleep turned solid.

Husbands

State Housing Area

1

The husbands are all out back. They inhabit
The hard light of domestic gardens.

How gaily in the sun's enamel
Their pastel houses flaunt possession!

Theirs is the ecstasy of breath made clay.
Their fingers drip with paint and flowers.

27

2

In the distance stand the empty frames
Of half-built houses. Such nakedness!

The hands of future husbands haunt them.
They crave our will. They stand apart

As huge and vacant as abandoned hoardings.
They freeze into themselves like caves.

A View from the Back-Steps

for Louis Johnson

Like little hospitals the houses spawn . . .
Your words. The weekend yawns. Chainsaws
startle the sparrows in that apple-tree

where your playway boy hung his doll to death.
Shades of a blackened soul! Next door
my neighbour views me through binoculars . . .

In a hundred years this street could be a slum.
We live for today but leave no room to move.
In a house of chairs the kids play dad and mum.

The Nose

The small man at the back of the bus,
Drunk, shrunk to a terrible pygmy size,
His face inverted, his loose mouth working
On words of bare-fanged wisdom, tipped
His six o'clock eyes towards me, blinked
Their poisoned lids, and cried
You bloody Jew, you hooked-nosed bastard,
You yellow fucking Ikey you! How
Did you get here you bastard? Mumbled
Should have been cooked at Buchenwald,
And spewed on his RSA badge. I
Am not a Jew, nor a Carthaginian,
Nor a Roman, nor a Norman,
Nor a brown-eyed bent-nosed Finn. In fact
I do not know who I am, and this
Sometimes gives me a headache. Still,
He knew me, he had me taped, he felt
Wholly definite and strong towards me.
My long nose stirred some sediment in him.
He faced a luxury too large for his taste.
He was on his guard, his flag unfurled,
His cry . . . *One land, one war, one nose.*
I turned in rage – but could not move
For, looking into his eyes, I saw
All life denied . . . my answering hate
Confined to some unspeakable void.

The Gods

On viewing emasculated Maori gods,
Dominion Museum, Wellington

Priapus has the smoothed-in crotch
of a camera blonde. He's trimmed to the Age.
Freud said we're afraid. He distrusted Gods.
They all came down to him from the cross
Begging for aid – then, behind his back,
Cried out *'More nails!'* Just like Gods
Once inside a man they feel caged.

Gods are afraid of men. Men have invented them.
When two Gods meet in the mind of man
One of them gets put away
In the back-room of a museum. Men
Howl for a chisel. A God has been caged.
There is something suddenly human about him.
They cut him back. He is less than a man.

The new God is a God of convenience.
The old God is a God of offence.
Who'd be a God? Alive or dead
They suffer most at the hands of men.

Three Poems from Plunket Street

for Louis Johnson

Just a word from one of our younger consumers . . .

Mum's got cramp in the hands. Those damned
squeeze bottles don't squirt themselves:
row after row pile up, and now
white plastic blinds her – she can't tell
fly spray from tomato sauce. Since
friday dad's had a pain in his groin
and won't sleep in the same bed. When
the doctor called I heard him mention sex
and something about four walls. Dad says
'those quacks are all pills and ink,
home's like being holed up in a trench.'
He was overseas in the war and knows
about strange diseases and the way wogs live:
I've heard him scream in his sleep . . .

                                      Oh yes

we've got a new concrete fence. Mum
pretends it will stop the neighbours' kids
from eating our blood and bone. I think
they're both exhausted. I don't envy them.

Dad's taken to booze and dreams of fair women . . .

I'm bombed. I just smiled at a police dog
turning its nose up at a lamp-post. That's
what I call training! Screw that cardboard blonde
winking through drizzle in the chemist's window.
Who makes them life-size? *Don't you understand*
what a useless stuck-up bitch you've become?
The Mrs would think she was lovely. Wouldn't
it kill you! All these nymphs and gods
glued behind glass, sipping dry martinis
and chewing pearls. Who lives like that?

If I gave the Mrs a fur bikini
she'd put it in moth balls. Nymphs and gods
are for men of leisure . . . poets and professors
and the blokes who make toothpaste. I know my lot.

Mum wears blue shoes to match her bruises . . .

and knits a sweater from my old socks.
She keeps crawling on our new cork tiles:
playing hop-scotch with a cube of ice
and singing freedom songs. I can't stand Belafonte!
She's always showing off – making out
I've taken to dope or raped the typist.
Come to think of it I've led a quiet life;
never harmed no one, never asked her for nothing.

Grumpy in the Department Store Window

Under everyone's feet I'm something less
than human . . . hence so loveable. (Forgive
a touch of malice but you'd never guess
how much of the soiled romantic's left
in your pet grouch.) Lautrec's
my patron saint. He'd sense
some of the irony, seeing me pegged
with lamp and spectacles beneath the legs
of Miss Teenage. Hey Ho! It's all
pure fiction, all beyond *my* reach. She
cools her thirst on Babychams
and sinks into pink silk sheets. At
our place it's soup and saveloys
and seven to a bed. (We've begged
the government for a State-House but

our morals stand condemned.) Outside,
a grey suburban sprawl; within,
a growing middle-age spread,
have taken toll. Snow White's grown cold;
full of good sense but no fun anymore.
On my days off I lie on the lawn
with a couple of plaster gnomes. I dream
of small clay goddesses with ample breasts.

The Man with the Carpet-Bag

I'm afraid of the man in the mural. The one
in the Trading Bank (dated 1840)

with his top-hat and his carpet-bag
and his talent for getting things going.

Everyone's playing grab with this bag-man.
They all insist he's one of the family.

Politicians point to his public gaze.
Generals say he stands like a howitzer.

His wife's more distant: borne above the surf
by happy Maoris with not a hand out of place

she's a bundle of pins and calico. It would take
a Botticelli to let down *her* hair, to paint

a plump Greek goddess coming over the waves
instead of this stiff-backed servant to his pleasure.

As he strides inland, raising guns and flags,
she sways uncertainly. Her thin grip tightens.

I tremble to think of all the carpet-bags
he's hauled ashore, still waiting to be opened.

Salvador Dali at the Hollywood Bowl

On the movie set intelligent tranquillized lions
purr like warm cameras. The swooning blonde,
sprayed a marigold bronze, sinks into her mould
of jungle mink. On a magnetized pillow
gold tresses arrange their rich molecules in waves.
The moist face of the director beams like a sunflower.

Padding home, past the used rocket lots
where ancient nose-cones gleam a cold pewter,
the lions yawn gold-plated dentures.
Somewhere, a black bat, impaled on a radar reflector,
emits small bleeps on screens in concrete caves.

In the creative stillness of the director's palace
lions crunch the cold leaves of frozen sunflowers.

Death of a Dog

Sally is dead, and the children stand around
like small white lilies. Someone,
in a terrible hurry, has ground
her red tongue into unaccustomed silence.
Now, all that was so much living
lies like a mound of wet rags, freezing
beneath my daughter's rough excited hands.

It is no risk for her, this going near
a silence she cannot understand.
Frank as forever she has wandered out
beyond all thought of our complaining
and stands there pouting, puzzled to believe
that one who partners her adventures
still lies at daybreak in a tangled sleep.

I tell her this is death, and leave
it at that. She doesn't weep
but runs repeating what she's learned
to all who'll listen. Women up the street
spare kindness – grief quickens them
like a cup of tea. Their men,
more urgently, cram early buses . . .

Life bursts into diesel oil and nicotine.
She feels her message meets with mild reproof
and so returns to that child-crowded scene
where all was black and white, but finds
someone's removed the death she runs to greet.
Tonight there'll be a burying, and tomorrow
a gap in the world to watch her cram with pleasure.

Mr Maui at Home with the Death Goddess

*Maui, the Maori hero, was crushed between the thighs of
the Death Goddess (a sleeping giantess) while attempting
to conquer Death by climbing into her womb and out
through her mouth.*

My children are killing me
Am I sick?
Where's my manhood?
Why don't you bring
Your sex in on a velvet cushion
Trimmed with black lace?
I like black
It's funereal . . . I'm not subtle
My children are killing me
I'm thin . . . They're fat
And full of complaints
They eat me up.

I'm possessed . . . The sea
Of your sex flows over us
I want it for myself
You send me forth
With shirt and sandwiches
I bring the sun home
Am I not a man?
I bring the sun home
Wrapped in sandwich paper
I unwrap it for you
It is dead . . . I sink
Into this nightly weariness.

What will become of us?
Even my brothers
Are clerks in a Tourist Office
Where is my net
That I caught the sun in
And fished up islands?
No islands are left, you say
What of ourselves?
Where is my jawbone club?
A fly-swat for the kitchen shelf!
Ah, how my head aches
To have your thighs comfort me . . .

Ah, how my mind cracks
Between your crossed legs!

Mr Maui Builds a New Office Block

I'm changing things. My yellow cranes
dangle office blocks or smash chained suns
on to your rotting wood. I push
whole streets aside – trees, benches, pubs,
old graveyards, all that dated
junk . . . KERUNCH! I'm hooked
on progress, on corridors of power,
sheer surfaces, neon sparkle, lifts
as big as buses, the whispered hush
of executive toilets. I'm creative.
I raise great ladders. I dangle the sun.

An Egyptian Immigrant Sells Insurance
in the Spring

Yes, Mr Osiris, we are 'only mortal'
but it's Spring not Autumn! OK, I agree
the sun still wrinkles our upturned faces
and none of us dance like gods in the street;
but Lambland's not all a vale of tears . . .
between the small print I can clearly see
your new brick villa and a station-waggon
packed with plump children, prize pumpkins, spilt seeds.

A Sonnet for Exiles

I praise all exiles, the Crusoes, Whittingtons,
Flying Dutchmen and Prodigal Sons
whose accents, flat-feet, or bloody-mindedness
kept them out of the village band.

I praise all those who weren't even wanted
by the third eleven, who never got cheques
to stay away from the family boardroom,
who left without flags or fond farewells

to build small lives in distant places
with only a chip on their backs. I point
to what States do best – sending off
the unwanted flotsam of their wars and debts,

that orphaned race who sail away to discover
the depths of their neglected grace.

An Exile in the House

*A young settler in New Zealand in the 1950s considers his
immigrant mother-in-law's past pride and present residence.*

1

Dear mother-in-law, your fare for 'home'
(sewn in a camphor-bag like holy bones)
weighs down my house. Being your landlord
is no joke . . . or is it? As a girl
you also packed your bags, a drab
north-country immigrant sailing south
with her adventurous cockney beau.
Why *did* that cool Dickensian cad

leave you marooned? (For thirty years
share a State-House in the colonies
then, growing old, go 'home' alone?)
The penny drops when your daughters swear
that all you'd wanted was a place of your own.

2

Being dumped at my door as an extra guest
with two pregnant daughters (one unwed)
is even worse for you than being short-changed
or walking in front of a white cat. You
once marched miles with bucket-and-soap
to shine the family car. You kept
the mop-head bright, rolled lawns, bore
daughters between starched sheets. At
nine each night you went to bed,
a settler's slave right up to the day
he packed his bags, yelling down the path
'I need company not a pair of boiled hands!'
So much for married men. Now you've made
my house your hermitage, your borrowed bed
a temple for ikons of your girls aged six.

3

Electricity is sex. Our lives
are all being taped. You wept today
for lost identities and try to blame
the change of life . . . or place . . . or name.
For thirty years you gave your all.
Betrayed, you praise *'real* gentlefolk'
who live abroad and never daub
their houses lolly-pink, like mine.
I praise the air's clarity and room to move
hoping that, somehow, light and space
may yet erase your inner pain. But

'something' you claim, in the climate here,
'eats us away,' makes us 'daft or mad.'
A tribal exhaustion perhaps? I lose my cool
and rage at your blatant distrust of facts.

4

This land evades you. You recall the past
in moral overtones – but your daughters laugh
at their gin-soaked grandad chopping up his chair
for firewood in an English mining town . . .
and on this side of the globe, at their own dad
selling up his home-museum
where the chairs were far too delicate
to be sat on, the clocks 'too antique'
to tell the time. At least
the neighbours haven't changed, all
'common filth' still . . . especially that clerk
who strips your youngest through binoculars
and snarls when my snails eat up his plants. One day
he'll axe us! When his anxious fingers
have hacked-out every border post
they'll creep into your sleep and sever
all your connections with a purer past.
You're scared, and I'm too much the vagrant
to wave some tattered Union-Jack. In fact
I'm 'in league with government spies'
who plot to sabotage your secret plans
for curtseying debutantes and snow-white weddings.
Too late! Your typist daughters swell
under my roof where all the rootless chaos
of the tribal outcast comes home to jest.

Landfall with Cannibals, Goats, and Mirrors

Waking, wet with light, I'm swimming
Naked in the bedroom mirror. Who's calling?
Land's in sight. Children yell
Like cannibals. It's me they're after!
The day looms over us. What a sandpile!
I crawl towards it through pygmy fingers.

It's all there, crammed in the open window –
The filling out of an old idea:
Hills round as mushrooms in the white of my eye
And the ocean flashing like a blue gorse fire.
I've sailed the night on creaking timbers.
Sprawled ashore, kids kick me alive.

I drag them to school past goats with yellow eyes
And leave them marooned before a blind black mirror.

House with Cat or Sun

a drawing by Jo, aged 4

An idiot sun, cross-eyed, smiles down
benevolence on a fist-full of windows
crammed into a house. A huge
three-legged cat is trying
to squeeze in through a floating door.

Or perhaps a malevolent cross-eyed cat
is jumping on to the roof
while a huge three-legged idiot sun
is floating *out* of the open door?

Or it could be a helicopter taking off
that has nothing to do with cat *or* sun
while a huge three-legged flower
grows outside the only window
in an idiot house crammed full of doors.

The Building

I'd like to live in your lap, said
my daughter. *And that* (my pocket)
is a door. She stepped
up from the ground floor of my toes, and began
the bony climb to where my backside spread
big as a boardroom on the sofa. Curiously
I was feeling about as bare as a public
building after work – that time
of being when light falls streaming
on to dust and detergents, when foreign women
slop out hidden mops. Chest-
high she stopped, knocking twice, and entered
ignoring the huge KEEP OUT sign (not
that she would lose her step
in that blackened inner smoke-room). It
wasn't guilt made me want to push
the stale jokes and dated pin-ups
out of her way, they just seemed dull – so
unforgivably monotonous when faced
by a true professional. *Go away*
I said. And she took the lift
back to the basement. She wasn't hurt
just bored with one so full of doors. These
days public buildings are all the same.

The Happy Army

The child has a vision of the happy army. He
has carefully sketched in my appointment book
the smiles, the fingers, the boots and guns
his happy army wave like rattles. No
one is dying, no one's bad or good,
and even the one at the back has a medal
while the generals beam pure love. The sun
has rolled to the ground, has been caught up
in a growing air of excitement that runs
riot, filling the sky with faces, arms, legs
and bits of old tanks. It is natural
that everyone, everywhere, faces the front,
not out of discipline or to scare the enemy
but in frank expectancy of applause. And
of course this is why this particular army
is happy, why no one dies, why the sun
shares in the happy army's happiness
and rolls down to earth. It is why I run
towards the boots and guns, why I come
as far as I dare to the edge of the paper
to stare . . . to stare and to cheer them on.

Poem at Pukerua Bay

This summer we've had two beached whales
(more dead than rocks). We wrote them off
as bits of the dark left over, midnight
ocean-offal, or pieces of black
horizon to be booted . . .
                          Light
is mineral hard; no mirages; my arm
clangs on your bikinied thigh.

Then how to live? As objects? Waking
out of what depths? (A glass of red wine
behind tight midnight doors; outside,
those two dead hills . . . no . . . caves.)

                      It's day!
The light lets nothing come between us.
We lie like fallen monoliths. The bay
is vacant now . . . there's only a brown man
with slabs of ocean on his back, and sticks
of eels that buckle like thin black drains.

Trains

Lying awake . . . suddenly . . . steaming
out of the dark the great trains came
over the bridge of my mind, wheels shaking.
Shaking, I crossed back again.
                                        Summer
and out of a blaze of steam
I pedalled into an old man's stare.
He'd been waiting for the trains forever
and laughed when I whistled like the first train
                                        . . . hurtling
over the rails of his gaze. He turned
and flung the fields out like a golden rug:
signals, rabbits, hills of ripe grain
leapt to the slam of train after train.

I tried to trail the tarred rails back
to the hole in the day where the trains came from
but bird-song, ponds that dropped from the sky,
even some bare arms in a summer loft,
called me aside
                        . . . waving with me
as the great trains passed.

The fields burnt black. Stars like moths
champed at the distance in the distance. Locked
in a speeding carriage I watched
children cheer and the fields fly off.
It was dark in the tunnel of the old man's stare.
How that frail bridge shook as we crossed!

Lying awake . . . suddenly . . . steaming
out of the dark the great trains came.

3

England
1974-1984

Paranoia in Piccadilly Circus

'To live in the city is to live inside oneself.'
— Claes Oldenburg

Broken glass in my doner kebab
and the big cars with their caps and flags
nudging me off the kerb. People

all have knives in their backs,
wigs, screams, and dirty macs. I run
to the Underground to phone Love up

but the telephone booths are glass coffins
stacked on their ends. The dead
are still dialling for a friend.

I'm lost. The escalators
run on and on. (They're made
by a firm called Piranesi.) Yobos

spray me with blood. (It's sold
in half-pint cans.) They write
THIS IS LIFE WITH A CAPITAL F

over my new white shirt. Scared,
I clench my fists and yell.
Immediately I'm signed up for *The Palladium*.

In these streets there's no escape.
Everyone wants to make a million.

Urban Living

Skylines change without warning.
Languages shift between streets.

New neighbours arrive in fleets of ambulances
carrying carpet bags and strange gods.

What's local is various but always carefully
'there' within arm's reach

though understandably one's sense of belonging
is sometimes less than secure. What we share

are the infinite facts of the everyday . . . light
trimmed to a leaf, bridges poised in mid-air,

all the bombs in the town square
endlessly ticking . . .

Mr Maui at Buckingham Palace

dumping the suit of armour my grandfather
was given by Queen Victoria. The fool
even wore it in bed. At the Governor's ball
he looked like Don Quixote. Now
I've chucked it back, over the palace wall.
True, the little Gurkha guard got shirty
but I gave him my black-power stare. You'll
notice I'm wearing my 'Pommie Bastard' T-shirt
and thumping stray bobbies with the jaw-bone club
I tore from an old whore's mouth. Lately
I've developed a sense of history . . .

this visit purges my colonial past.
Soon I'll be looking for a girl to crawl into.
Someone my type . . . a goddess perhaps.
I don't like debs. They're always crossing cool legs.
I like my women wide open. I can't speak fairer than that.

Mr Maui at the Marbella Beach Club

All these smooth limbs, these exquisite shrubs,
and this blue pool going on and on . . .
It does something to me. Chilled
glasses start to crack in my grip.
My skin soaks up sun-oil like a sponge.

I've lived too long in the dark perhaps?
Suddenly I'd like to run amok. I've got
forty-eight hours on someone else's bill.
I'm a god with an overpowering need
to forgive myself for something I haven't yet done!

Mr Maui on the Way to the Film Studio

Here's me in my milk-white Rolls
scattering the peasants. I've signed up
to play the part of myself in a dream
of how this bastard from a broken home
became a god. Even so
I'm in hock to the bigger gods
they keep behind closed doors . . .
                                        Look

through this tinted window just

how delicate the world is. Tree
and hedgerow, field and pond,
are quickened by speeding glass.
Sky-Father, I still feel your hand
in the ecstasy of my casual glance.

A Consideration of the Tao at the
Kingston Labour Exchange . . .

where the poets and peasants
and out-of-work carvers
of ivory and jade
gather to discuss the decline of capitalism
and the ironies of personal fate.

                          Outside, in the rain
and late October wind, Lao-Tse
leaves his Chinese Take-Away
to begin his last long journey
in a '57 Ford. We rush
to the window to wave him off . . .
a happy, selfish, mild old man
leaving his family and his debts
and heading, once more, for the hills.

Chancellor Schmidt at Chequers –
Winter 1978

The Chancellor plucks a flower from the wall.
The cameras are purring. It is bitterly cold.
The Chancellor is wearing gloves.
He feels the cold more than the flower does.
His face is ageless, like Pharaoh's or God's.
The Chancellor pauses to smell the flower.
Perhaps he'd rather smell flowers than talk
about money and wars behind closed doors.
Perhaps that *was* a flicker of sadness
crossing his face as they led him away
still smelling the flower, still looking back
at the winter sunlight and the flowerless wall.

Bel-Air Primitive

A neighbourly sherbet fountain coats
this barbed-wire fence with sugar-loaf. It
glints and tinkles. Greek garden nymphs
are painted *Playboy* centrefolds –
black pubic hair, red plastic tits.

Next door slim pink flamingoes pick
an exiled banker's lawn for bits
of lobster bisque. When curved beaks hit
old booby traps these birds explode
like soft pink sunsets over pink gins.

On darkening hills gold golf-carts chase
white atoms into space. O
endlessly the perfect tee-shots click
like Vegas chicks going down the strip
in high-heels with the lights ablaze.

Moving On

I like this house. It's warm working-class Gothic.
But lately the walls have begun to close in.
Someone keeps peeing through the letter box.
I'm snowed under with pamphlets, petitions, bills.
Everyone has a cause: even the postman recalls
A sense of belonging to Churchillian years
When only landmines littered the hall.

Outside, the tower-blocks are on the move again;
Burglar alarms buzz like battery hens;
Hospitals take to the streets. Last week
I was mugged by a ten-year-old
Then run over by the meals-on-wheels.
As I pack my bags another letter explodes . . .
The batons are out again! Banners sway down the road!

Up There

Forty storeys high, above the noise and dust,
twilight ripens: penthouse windows flash
their splendid isolations through the dusk.

Like Draculas the old tycoons wake up
as hushed lifts bring them nude Miss Worlds.
Between the stars small helicopters dash

with polar martinis, Rembrandts, fresh
silk shirts. In gold wheelchairs
these pale recluses salve their secret hurts.

Their visitors are others like themselves –
mad millionaires who bathe in milk,
scrawl fat cheques on human flesh,

sleep in their spats on starched black sheets.
Dying, these ancients vanish like Viking Chiefs . . .
their private jets burn out across lost lakes.

Then, towers tremble. Down basement steps
they drag some playboy with two broken legs
(he'll swear it happened at St Moritz). Weeping

he waves to the press. His lift ascends.
The golden wheelchairs claim another King.

On Government Lawns

Fat peasants hurl their Gucci bags
in the faces of the press. Country
cousins are new here. They'll soon learn.
Only last week they were dressed in rags
and crawling across parched fields. How
elegant the generals' wives are! And
the generals themselves are trying so hard
to be decent and well-bred. At least
one can't hear the screams in the palace yard
above the massed murmur of string quartets.
And the doves are lovely. (Except
for the dead ones.) Whole
container-trucks full of peace! On
government lawns past Presidents
are playing golf with some refugees.
How happy the old statesmen are
now that the assassins are somewhere else!
They wave their clubs and weep. In
a rush of patriotism at the champagne bar
two bodyguards shoot each other
through the knees. It's a farce of course –
but on such a scale! When the handshakes cease
bodies are piled up house-high in the streets.

Out of Season

Something is about to happen
at the Hotel du Lac. Mussolini's aunt
still visits out of season.
She's served by six waiters in a ballroom
with cracked lakeside windows.
Broken boats anchor above the Parma ham.

Local blue-blood is down to one
arthritic bishop, and a countess
who's turned her summer palace
into a children's camp. Coach-trips
from Chicago crunch their truffles;
trucks, smashing the pavements, rumble past

full of lire for Swiss banks.
(It's the only time the chandeliers dance.)
After lunch Mussolini's aunt
plays cards with the hotel gardener
who once ran a brothel in Milan.
That's the fun of these outdated places –

what's about to happen already has.
We gaze at lakes and mountains
as abandoned as ourselves.
Far off in Hong Kong and Katmandu
the rich are thinking of coming back.
They dream again of Palladian mansions,

rococo fountains, dying swans,
all the old décor of a decadent Europe
tarted up for the lads. Meanwhile
the towels are rarely changed,
the trains run late, and Mussolini's aunt
beats the gardener at five-card stud.

This Way to Samarkand

Whenever I'm broke and grubbing around
for the price of a pint, I think
of James Elroy Flecker who wrote
anything to pay the bills –
tourist blurbs, trade journal guff –
writing it with a will and in
a white shirt because that way
he might get hired again. Not
a popular man (having no influence)
and a bit of a stay-at-home – but
in the few hours he won for himself
then to hell with bangers and mash and
yahoo to the local literati! Keeping
his head in the clouds he built
the entire city of Samarkand. No one
knocked on those doors with a bailiff!
And so, whenever I'm broke, I join
James Elroy on his elephant-clouds
heading east over the roofs of the town
with the sunlight streaming through our empty hands
and our wives and children swaying at the back.

Nodding Off

Witness the demise of this fantastic ego,
the thickening of the body, the sky in its head
clouding over for an after-party, over-forty
nod in the sprawling kingdom of itself. Regard
the slack mouth that can bawl like a baby,
rage, suck, desire, put its bones
in a glass, and the heavy chest –

now slumped – that in ecstasy
howls for love and holds its breath,
and the nose, monolithic, a towering crag
the limbs look up to . . . magnificent!

It's the mushroom season, early Autumn,
a whole kingdom is crumbling, a dictatorship
at the height of its powers but over-spent,
over-grown, over-indulgent, with a hint
of rebellion in the sewers and the borders
beginning to lose themselves. But the legs
bulge, the blood drums up
its sleeping legions, and a wine-stained tongue
taxes the provinces for the last of their wealth,
and the heart leaps with a new malevolence
and forgives and forgives and forgives itself!

Here comes that childhood pond again . . .

with cows on stunted stilts
and insects walking like Christ on water.

Fish leap screaming into my hands.
I swallow them. I eat streams and forests.

Ditches! How I love green ditches!
They hide me. They go nowhere . . . lovingly.
Somewhere, always, boats are hooting

so I run up the gangplank at the end of the street
where liners are parked like enormous coffins.

Immigrants, tourists, refugees . . .
Guns go off! Bands are playing.

Everyone wants to be somewhere else.
There's a rush for uniforms, countries, profit.

Sailing away like Kings and Queens
hordes of dead parents are smiling and waving.

Bear Dance

for Beryl

To bring you to my bed
I must dramatize myself:
I must walk through the house
in primary colours.

How else can I be seen
among all the children and flowers
among all the music and mirrors
among all the open windows
that surround us?

I have to shout
to wear bright shirts
to dance up and down
rattling the cups in the kitchen.

The children laugh.
They say I'm a bear.
They like it best when I roll on the ground.
They say there's a dancing bear in the house.

But this is my love dance.
Aheee . . . I bellow . . .
clicking my throat like the starlings
in the early morning
when they think they've swallowed the sun.

This, I say, is my love dance.
Later I shall paint your image.
There'll be a bold but awkward tenderness
trembling in each line . . .
I'll be struggling to overcome my clumsiness
with the strength of my love.

These are my charms –
my bear dance and my image of you.
With these I'll bring you to my bed
again and again.

When you see me in my bright shirt
when you hear neighbours and friends complaining
saying I'm loud and heavy-footed
remember that my dance is for you.
It's in your sole honour.
It has to compete with your silence
and with the other silences that go on and on
like the sky through this open window
for ever . . .

At Kensal Green Cemetery

No joke, this weight of stone, these
gothic monoliths with granite scrolls –
clerics and Raj-men, Victorian bosses
in tombs as magnificent as their homes.
Good neighbours all (one race and blood)
secure in their Englishness even in death –
poets no one ever reads, generals
who'll never relax their grip.

                            And these
in an open patch of earth
next to the main road, far
from sheltering trees – Mr Rajneesh,
Calypso Pete, Harry the Greek, Armenian Joe,
with wedding photos in plastic bags
and flowers in cans among gravel chips
that rattle like seeds as lorries pass.

Notes for the Park-Keeper

They've put the park bench
too near the pond. Lovers could drown
if the drains backed up. There's
a touching Chinese look to the plants
bordering the council flats. Perhaps
the gardener's a Buddhist but
he's far too trusting. His bamboo patch
has been flattened into a speedway track
for chopper bikes. That bench

sometimes doubles as a raft. Kids
use it to fish for eels. They get
twenty pence each from *Prestos* so
they climb the railings at night
to gaff by flashlight and to carve
graffiti into the picnic logs –
DUFFY FOR CHELSEA . . . NIG-NOGS
GO HOME . . . and, strangest of all,
PICASSO PAINTS WITH HIS COCK.

*

The park's Victorian wrought-iron gates
are beginning to look like a cage
(shades of old 'class barriers'). That
and the bandsmen's buttoned-up uniforms
(deck-chairs in regimental rows)
gives the place a nineteenth-century ambience

that stiffens each evening as shadows spread
heavy gothic lines. A picket fence
could be less inhibiting
while a sprinkling of violins and bare arms
might add a small bohemian gesture
to the bandstand's blatant military blare.

*

Water's essential to the public's sense
of nature at peace with itself.
It's what we expect to see –
air, water, light, all meeting here
in 'a marriage of earth and sky.'

The fountain's gone in the new council cuts –
which limits both ear and eye
(and how the tongue loved something cool
coming straight out of the ground). But
if they pruned the plane trees further back

63

then a view of the river would linger on
past Harrod's Depository – the one
with domes and union-jacks
that houses a dusty Empire
of forgotten furniture and cabin trunks.

At Dawn the Thames is the Ganges in Flood . . .

and Mr Rajneesh bathes his hands and feet
as the day sails in through Hammersmith bridge
like a scarlet dhow trailing light.
He's accompanied by his sacred hound –
the one that guards his curry shop.
It's six in the morning. There's something oceanic

about this river at dawn. Mr Rajneesh
leaves his jacket folded
and rolls his trousers up to his knees.
He washes neatly, submerging his dog,
splashing their flesh till it stings.

Smoke from a boatsmith's sawdust pyre
drifts downstream. There's the smell
of live mud. Mr Rajneesh moves off
just as a milkfloat hums through the mist
like a single, silent, large white cow
clinking its collar of glass beads.

Thames Talk

1

High tide and the Thames in flood
maroons our flat among office blocks
like floating pagodas. Below
are rivers of drowned trucks.
I'm on the fourth floor reading Chuang Tzu
who loved water. A passing yacht
fails to stop at a pedestrian crossing
and heads for the British Home Stores.

It's the Spring Equinox. Life's rushing back
but a damp population is out of touch.
Only the old in the park line up
their deck-chairs with that gap in the clouds
where the sun disappeared last year.
(They hug libations of weak tea
and patiently wait for a mildewed band
to blow away this fog.) There's a hush

as the tide turns and something eternal
tugs at its moorings. (Chuang Tzu
falls from my hands.) A boat-
load of lost Japanese tourists
refuse to panic as their engine stops.
They turn, en masse, to face due East
and slowly vanish into the mist.

2

Weekend crowds cram the Putney pubs
with sounds of breaking glass and loud
transistor howl. A week
of jungle heat has melted
the Chelsea Pensioners' wax moustaches.
Pot-bellied pickets strip off and stroll

like lonely beauty queens
beside locked wharves. Tides bring
a touch of lost horizons – sea
smells, stray gulls, that sudden hush
of light on water that Turner flogged
from Claude's sad cities with their 'rosy dawns'

but it's mostly Babylonian visions
of crumbling council-blocks, or no-go lawns
where merchants gather behind high walls
among debs and summer tents. Dogs,
wandering the tow-path, ignore all calls
and bugger each other like perfect gents.

Tidal Fields – Chidham

This is no landscape for a tidy mind:
the sea insinuates, trundling mud
into our inland barn. All night,
though attic-high, we've heard
salt waters lapping underground . . .

A vision of the flood, you smile, *a dream
common after love*. We talk
of great whales leaping and hazel forests
bending forked branches down to earth.

You are my love diviner, listening close
to midnight womb-talk with a moony grin.
Our bodies flow. Our tongues lick salt.
How I love this place where earth and water meet!

Where doves and gannets mingle in the trees
and loaves and fishes populate the fields.

Lines during Convalescence

'No one seems to know
How useful it is to be useless.' – Chuang Tzu

1 *Still Life*

I love touching domestic surfaces . . .
an apple, a vase, a limb.
I gorge on the small excitements
of material things.

I like white walls with windows
but I don't stare out:
I let the windows stare in.
I try to become a still life.

Still lifes are never really still.

2 *Shhh! I'm becoming a republic*

I like locked doors, walled
gardens, secluded
patios where the sunlight's trapped.

Inside my head there's a moat.
It's taken years to build.
Only ants can cross it, stray butterflies,

and my Lady – who comes
with doves to hand. Love
is a long convalescence. I can see

moths coupling above the clouds.
I can hear worms writhing underground.
I'm becoming a Republic.

It won't last. Outside my
softly crumbling walls
the legions gather and the scoutcars prowl.

Poems for Jo

Listening

with a microphone plugged into the earth.
We can hear ferns creaking, rabbit-chatter,
beech-roots muscling up through the dirt.

We can hear bones turning, bees spawning,
mushrooms growing, ants drinking sap.
When we take our earphones off we can hear

earth's huge silence listening back.

Night Hound

This pile of old white wool called dog
is slack and soft. He smells
like stale crumbs
or a dishcloth left in the sun. Ants
tickle his pink pig-belly, midges
dine on his eyes, his stiff stick legs
swim sideways through sleepy whimperings.
Nothing shakes him out of his skull.

Come evening he creaks to his feet.
Petals fall from his tongue. Earth's
suddenly the colour of his own blood
but cooler. He watches sun
sink like a big bone in yellow mud.
Then he's off, snapping at stars. In
the dark between two blades of grass
herds of small spiders scratch and thump.

Blackberrying

Late summer. Let's see if they're ripe.
Let's hide in torn thickets
where the big ones shine
high up in the light – black suns
to be plucked from the sky. Let's dine
among bees and blue flies, buckets
bubbling red – earth's blood
slopping over the sides. Let's suck

those plump clusters free of their shape,
hands scratched, tongues purple again, limbs
wrapped in long thorns that tug at our clothes,
holding us close to the ground among bones,
bottles, sweet smelling mould,
and a damp grass no one mows.
Let's go home with seeds in our teeth
and a dark taste in our throats.

Water-Mad

Left in the garden
with bucket or hose
we're water-mad.
We like to watch it pour
into the light
and over cupped leaves.

Earth has no mouth
but it sucks water in
through the dry pores of its skin.
Then, grass stiffens, petals wave
newly laundered flags, beaks
bend to the scent of something damp.

We pour and pour
until night flows
out of the air, until our toes
are drowned in darkness,
until our hands
grow into the ground they soak.

A breeze through bees' fur . . .

and a mist when you lift small stones:
dead things there, a scrabbling,
a shine on the backs of the unborn.

Just Looking

1 *Bonnard at Le Cannet – 1942*

There'll be no more cod Lautrecs
or fashionable graphics for friends in Paris.
Here, in the south, his vision sweats:
ladies at tea in frills and blue bonnets
blatantly ache to lick cream
from their fingers.
              But his wife
(over sixty by now) won't pose so
he draws her from memory. She never ages.
Year after year she stands there naked
as pert as on the day they met. The trick
is in keeping her young, in painting
back her beauty each day with such passion
that even death feels compelled to wait;
stopping off to buy grapes, or adjusting
a particularly smart straw hat
before knocking.

2 *Viewing Primitives*

In the best work nothing's willed:
everyone shares a sense of occasion
and the proper self-esteem. People
seem to be in fancy dress (wedding groups,
clean children, minor government officials)
but this is simple reportage . . .
though god knows where it could lead.

As witness one scene where Rousseau picks up
some solitary leaves. These
tempt him to visit the botanical gardens
where jungles are suddenly commonplace
and where his neighbour's unobtainable nude wife
can be safely arranged on a studio couch
among artistic tigers and edible flowers.

3 *So Late in the Day*
The paintings of Claude Lorraine

Journeys, as metaphors, usually require
a crowd to cheer the hero off
but in Claude's great landscapes
no crowds gather – although
occasionally a passing cow looks up
at Perseus or the Queen of Sheba
embarking at sunset from an abandoned lot.

There's a furtive air about their going,
a proliferation of cloaks and hoods
and a sense that Claude's Arcadian ruins
are a dream dropped into after lunch,
a vision of man's 'golden past'
that acts as stage-set for what really matters,
this setting-out along an unknown path
so late in the day, with darkness falling,
at a time when most of us step back.

The Crusoe Factor

1 *Crusoe's Return*

The claustrophobia of cobbles,
mobs ruling the streets,
prim family faces
gossiping over tea.
And this cold –
it sharpens the arrow left
like an icicle in my knee.

Friday's swathed
in frost-fringed furs
like an eskimo or expensive whore!
You can't take him anywhere;
youths throw stones,
dogs howl, matrons scream.

Missing these streets
I tore my hair out,
moaned in my sleep,
raged at the sun . . .
Now I squint through latticed windows
kept firmly bolted against the stench.

2 *Mrs Crusoe's Complaint*

He's not the same man
since he returned. I blame it
on that black . . . bad
company that keeps him from
his own kind and class. The sun
too, has addled his brains.
He used to be a literary man
handy with a quip or pun
but now he laughs at 'mannerists'

who groan at his occasional grunts.
'God,' he told the vicar,
'is a blink in the eye of something big.'
Talk like that leads him to live
like an exile in his own land.
He'll walk the docks
for hours, but indoors
insists on doing all his own chores.
He'll cook, sew, light the fire,
sleep with the dog by an open stove.
What he wants from me god knows!
He shames me with his silences,
won't visit relatives or go to church.
How can he call himself an Englishman?
He's only happy when newly marooned.

3 *Crusoe's Lament*

A freak, a walking sideshow,
but at least Man Friday's not in chains.
Offers from a brothel in *The Shambles*
I turned down flat. My 'pet slave'
was all the rage until he shot
some 'pigeons' from the madam's hat!
Now we're dangerous heretics . . .
pimps or spies or something cursed.
(The devil's brood! Not cloven-hooved
but strolling in bare feet
through arcades.) Fear
keeps us indoors, more cut off
than on our island where, at heart,
we'd settled down for life – until
my 'Ship Ahoy!' let history in
and dropped us back in time.
(One smudge of sail against that blue
spreading like a gale!)
He shares my fate but pays his way

as artists' model, doomed to pose
for *Mythic Man* or *Before the Fall*,
his Horn-of-Plenty shrivelling with age.

4 *Crusoe on Whitby Sands*

This was always a coast for loners
with its ruined abbey and hermit's cave.
From here each age sent out its explorers
and gave a role to no-hopers
without friends at court. But always
behind the public voyage
lay what wasn't logged – a light that hurts,
midnight landfalls, the body's thirst . . .

Friday in a grass skirt, skin like black silk.
(Today he's a dithering grey-haired dolt!)
Friday by firelight, salt on his limbs,
green parrots crooning in the orange groves.

5 *Crusoe's Farewell*

Yesterday we took ship and sailed
towards the mouth of the sun.
Convicts, packed in mouldering hulks,
cheered as Friday jigged for joy
stark naked before the missionary band!
(My wife will find my farewell note
under my wig and folded clothes.)
Far beyond the fat Spice Isles
and distant colonies of gold and blood
we'll come again to that island home
that so mysteriously has chosen us.

4

New Zealand
1985-1990

Beginnings

Guthrie-Smith in New Zealand 1885

Who am I? What am I doing here
alone with 3000 sheep? I'm
turning their bones into grass. Later
I'll turn grass back into sheep.
I buy only the old and the lame.
They eat anything – bush, bracken, gorse.
Dead, they melt into one green fleece.

Who am I? I know the Lord's my shepherd
as I am theirs – but this
is the nineteenth century; Darwin
is God's First Mate. I must keep
my own log, full of facts if not love.
I own 10,000 acres and one dark lake.
On the seventh day those jaws don't stop.

Who am I? I am the one sheep
that must not get lost. So
I name names – rocks, flowers, fish:
knowing this place I learn to know myself.
I survive. The land becomes
my meat and tallow. I light my own lamps.
I hold back the dark with the blood of my lambs.

Just Passing Through . . .

for Louis Johnson, Pukerua Bay

1

'So are we all,' you say,
and seem a frank outsider still
among the hordes of company men
who spill from the plane
like plastic trays. 'Places
are people.' You again. These days
those few who touch us live
like *little lights*
across Siberias of space. Twelve
years away! I let the light sink in.

2

Imagination brings us down to earth
but 'belonging' isn't *just* roots put in,
it's fences falling, fields with no edge,
a looking up that lifts the heart into vagrancy
and leaves it breathless with nomadic bliss.

Your house does this . . . 'Kiwi Domestic'
it echoes to bare feet, laughter, kids.
It keeps an open door where
skies drift in and far waves spill
their blue infinities; where hills
and hills   and hills   and hills
solidify a silence thick as fur.

3

A girl in bikini and black sou'wester
dares the changeable evening air.
Everywhere the scent of fennel,
crushed by sun and rain, exudes

the sweetness of lost youth. I fed
three kids on berries, mushrooms, fish
filched from this stark bay. Since then
trees have tamed these windy slopes
and shelter pumpkins, maize, and grapes.
New houses huddle where mushrooms pushed
their skulls up through the mist.
The poets still live on their lonely crags
but grow begonias on their window-sills.

4

'Hang on tightly, let go lightly'
is a travelling clown's
or wandering Sufi's trick. To share
your lifelong interest in
an inner alchemy, helped widen a vision
stunted by immigrant loneliness.
Our flag was a hopelessly ragged map
of *Universal Man*, pinned
to that same door we slammed
when trapped by clichés of 'domestic bliss'.
These hills that lift our eyes to heaven
are the same as those that hemmed us in
back in prim Hutt Valley days
when 'letting go' was simply getting pissed.

5

Journeys: the hero setting forth
not knowing if he'll ever return . . .
Suburban man, more certain, clings
to his strap on this morning train
with its hooter like some ferry
on the Styx. A grim
mixed company . . . brollies, books, toupees,
and a ten-year-old who thinks he's boss
of some Flash Gordon game . . . Zap! Zap!

He fires his ray-gun across the bay
and watches a whole city crash.
Memories of drunken streets that sway
flood me with an old despair. ESCAPE
was always our coward's theme. ESCAPE and RAGE.

6

Your Chinese vase with its earthy glaze
seems quietly at home when placed
on any shelf. It travels well . . .
better than mere flesh. (I'd guess
it's the first thing you unpack.)
I drag my jet-lag into bed
and listen to the darkness crouch
like something solid round the house.
Such stillness hems me in, until
the quick light stings my eyes awake.
These deep simplicities of white and black
cut through my sense like an axe.
Our talk is quickened. All things must pass.
Your Chinese vase moulds silence like a last.

7

A ten-year absence leaves the prodigal
less than needed when he's back.
Habitual changes of wife or country
narrow to a lonely space
where exiles end up
talking to themselves. Blake –
exiled by his vision – invented
the art of looking two ways at once.
I envy his balancing of earth and heaven,
of dark and light, without
within. Two countries
split me down the middle. One
where I 'came from', and this
where I first learned to live.

8

Back in England ('a dated, droll,
unfashionable provincial place')
you found – inwardly cramped – a sort
of gentleness that 'ran rich and deep'
though the poets were 'hopelessly
middle-class'. You heard
something in Hughes's voice you liked;
something 'religious but abandoned'. You
told me once, when whisky rotten,
that the only gods left 'were lost but local'.

9

Time to leave. I pack my case.
Your child – a traveller too – escapes
through the garden fence you've raised
to keep her safe. She runs
to the sea where darkness thickens
(towards the distance in the distance)
towards some sense of self that takes her
away from all she loves. I know
I haven't far to go
compared to her fresh voyage. Back 'home'
the arms I crave are raising blinds
on bleak March days. It's Autumn here.
The first stars glow like small campfires.

Advice to Immigrants

'Over there, that's where your roots are.
Over there, in the air . . .' – Paul Celan

For the rest of your life
there'll be two sets of voices –
those in the street
and those in your head.
When they meet
you'll be 'at home'. (How quickly
your children learn another tongue!)

In the meantime take hold,
live by sight and touch,
offer yourself as a gift.
What else have you got?
You travel light.
You only have *your* hands, *your* eyes.
If your hosts turn away when you speak

that's alright. They have other
more established tasks. Your
traveller's excitement with the everyday
is something they've grown beyond.
Those whales at the end of the street,
eels in the drains, the lemon tree's
buttery flames . . . these

are commonplace. Don't worry when
the locals decline to jump up and down
at every 'new' sound or scent:
left alone, remember that we all
have our spiritual ancestors – those
who came before you; before them. In the end
history is on everyone's side . . .
or no one's, which is the same thing.

I.m. Ronald Hugh Morrieson,
New Zealand Novelist

A boxed-in animal fear rattles past
that prim green villa where you taught guitar
and pianoforte with all the skill
of a slaughterman's bored wrist.
(How many dairy-fed Lolitas
leaned to your keyboard's yellow grin?)

On the mantel the clock's monotonous tick
licked at the whisky in the rolltop desk.
No wonder you saw red. It was there
wherever you looked . . . bleeding hearts
on the kitchen wall, lips
smeared at the local dance. The clang

of a firetruck or a magpie's mad
sexual cackle, often broke the calm
that settled like dust on the sunday meringues
your mother loved to suck. Outside . . .
Mt Egmont's frosty tit
and the little tight towns clenched like fists.

Gauguin in Auckland 1891

I'm stuck in a swamp called *Freemans Bay*.
(The ship for Papeete will take ten days
to repair a propellor blade. We ran
into some whales.) My host
is a mad Parisian who claims
he invaded this place with a couple of brigs
over fifty years ago. He's ga-ga,
nearly ninety, and gives
piano lessons to the daughters of the rich.

'I won't,' he raves, 'go home
out of shame . . . I surrendered
in two days.' I explain
that no one in Paris gives a fig.
He bawls like a child. A goddess lives
on the far horizon whose womb's the sun.
I'm ten days late for her bed. Downstairs
a white-frocked schoolgirl murders Liszt
while my host beats time with her parasol.

Aunt Alice at the Alhambra
– Ponsonby 1943

They had usherettes in Turkish slippers
and Persian tiles in the loo. Coming
in by tram with some Yank, and then
strolling through those Ali Baba doors
'was like entering Paradise.' She smoked
OPIUM with new cork tips, and painted
black seams on her bare white thighs.
Glenn Miller played twice at the old *Three Lamps*

where she jitterbugged on the sawdust floor.
Dolores del Rio sang *Jealousy* there
and drunkenly boasted that Gary Cooper
'could go all night and was hung like a horse.'
'Life,' Alice said, after peace was declared,
'was never the same again. Then
everyone worked as government clerks
and the post-war years stretched on and on
like an endlessly boring five-year plan
or silent visits from the Plunket Nurse.'

Climbing down from Art-Deco Drive . . .

on 39 wooden steps, we passed
John Buchan's ghost in a Thirties Ford,
cream slacks, and Cairo brogues.
Upstaged by his perfect sense of style
we waved our summery but slovenly goodbyes
before dropping down towards a light
(reflected up from the sea) that seemed
even now, after so many years,
to promise 'an impartial bliss'
or, at least, an elemental stance. We'd
left that onwards-and-upwards path
where Mrs Miniver strolled with her dog
through two or three World Wars, and were
greatly relieved when the last few steps
left us naked, ankle-deep in mud,
with 'nothing more to our names'. John
Buchan waved at us, heading out
in his twin De-Havilland towards the sun
and dipping his silver wings as he passed.

Sunset with Blind Alleys and Hills

'To bathe objects in light
is to merge them with the infinite' – *Leonardo da Vinci*

Squeezing between venetian blinds
this orange sunset even outshines
the cartoon on TV. (That too
has a cloudy brilliance
against which Pluto's innocence
heroically shines forth.) In
both, as always, the sublime arrives
with Turneresque intimations
from the source.
                              Take
Pluto's scenes . . . the background grows
ever more mysterious. That
stile, for instance, that curve
in the road, those paths,
blind alleys, sunlit streams . . .
where do they lead? Drenched
in a dying sky such details
soon outgrow their narrative. It's
the same off-screen . . . a chipped sugar bowl
catches the light and earns its place
with a sweetness all the more moving because
no one meant to upstage Pluto's tricks
or pretend that this pause between day and night
was anything more than a breathing space.

Let's Meet . . .

between Flora's Massage Parlour
and The Temple of Higher Thought
where three motorways converge before veering off
downtown or 'out into the world'. I'll be wearing
my Sixties jeans and Elvis Presley loafers
and carrying your favourite carpet-bag –
the one with the canvas cottage.

Bring your old blanket with its mixed aroma
of ancient Kashmir and newly crushed fennel . . .
the one with 'moonlight intimations of Eden' –
remember? Come in the evening
so we can look back at the city
in that hush just before dark when Rangitoto
floats like a mermaid in her bush-clad bikini.

Where we'll end up is anyone's guess
but, once again, an infinite longing
tempts me to put on my best Chagall face
and whistle sad tunes on windy street corners
in the hope you'll see through this thin
disguise called Age, and call out my name
and beg me to praise your beauty.

Come In

The sea does, almost, and the moon would
if only it hadn't got stuck on the roof
and certain summery insects nearly make it
battering on the window-glass,
and a cat, black (not ours) that pads
the fenceline, an Egyptian hieroglyph
on four firm sideways paws. Shutters
and doors are wide open, hoping
for as many ghosts, guests, naked elements,
as one small domestic setting can get
perched 'at the edge of the world' and blessed,
as the man said, 'with fine northern slopes
and a bay at the end of the street.'
                                    And so
I think of New York (where I've never been)
and everyone being swallowed up
by those huge man-made canyons Mama Cass
used to sing about in the Sixties. It's
amazing what richness arrives when
one's feet aren't 'firmly planted' but
spread out like a well-darned net to catch
whatever the breeze brings in. The cat
looks up and knows I'm not there, moths
champ at the furniture, and *someone*
who's stepped about a yard outside of me
sits like a city by Max Ernst
happily forsaken
basking in his endless ignorance.

New Baptized

An English missionary is sent to pacify
a Maori Chief: New Zealand, 1850.

1

An island fortress. Some Yankee whalers
camp outside the Pa. (I noticed
several half-caste children.) It was
almost dark when we arrived:
a purple light staining the ocean
as though the sun had been harpooned.

The Chief received me cheerfully:
a War-Lord, small, beaked like a gull
but something disturbing
in his gaze. You can't see
into his thoughts. Dead
flesh was everywhere . . . arms . . . legs . . . skulls:

they eat their enemies for days. The Chief
tapped his teeth with a whalebone club
and laughed when I complained. He's
Anti-Christ. He turns blood
into wine; flesh
into unbaked bread. He keeps

his favourite greenstone axe
in a bible-box the Governor sent.
(He's burned the bible.) I'll not forget
this island, shaped like a stranded whale
(and smelling like one) rearing up
out of an ocean streaked with red.

2

I'm trapped in this knacker's yard. My bed
is next to the women's hut. They say
they want to warm my bones –
like David in old age! The Chief
has a growing appetite for Saul
and the slaughter in Chronicles. Christ

is not to his taste – except
for the crucifix. During Lent
he nailed some slaves to a log. They
took three days to die. On the fourth
he ordered them to walk. When
that failed he cut off their legs.

I was made to roll a stone across
the entrance to their cave. He's mad.
He sat all night in a mountain stream
to cure himself of the pox. He's asked
the Governor to let me stay. (They're
afraid in Wellington he'll raid

the coast.) I'm more a hostage
than a guest. Government House, as
usual, are out of touch. (Too much
crinoline and lace!) They write
to thank me for my 'civilizing gift'.
I'm Jester to an Old Testament King.

3

The warriors dance – like David naked
before his people. There's joy
in their limbs. They quote God's words:
'Slay man and woman. *Go and destroy*
infant, suckling, ox and ass.' I'm
Samuel, dressed in a goatskin. There's

blood on my collar and on my hands.
I moan for these dark Shumanitte women.
Lust foams at my mouth. Hine-nui-te-po . . .
their Death Goddess . . . lives on the horizon.
All journeys end between her thighs.
They bring me virgins, Hine's handmaidens:

I startle the sentries with my cries.
The warriors smile. They hear
my bed creaking. *That's Hine,'*
they grin. But I'm new baptized.
I bathe in Bathsheba's sweat. My
strength is as the strength of the Lord!

Letters Home – New Zealand 1885

for Allen Curnow

1

Flocks away, packed tight against the rails.
We boil them down for soap. Each
ewe's worth fourpence for her fat alone:
twice what we'd get by shipping them back home.
(How patiently they wait, heads bowed
like girls at Sunday School.) I try
to catch up on my notes
describing specimens of plant and stone
picked up on my walks. We hacked
cross-sections from live Kauri trunks
before we burned the slopes. I hope
to show them at Kew that decent work's being done
out here in the colonies. The smell
of blood and melting bones
fouls the verandah where I smoke.

(My notes on fault-lines are especially good.)
The lake's almost dried up. It's been
like Africa this year. The black
swans die in hundreds, eating
their own yoke. Eels
glut the crimson mud for scraps
tipped from the vats. I've seen
them crawl across the lawn
to grab a live sheep's foot. At night
I read the psalms . . . *'The Lord's
my Shepherd.'* It's most apt. Two
years here now. It almost feels like home.

2

Dear *friend* (there's no one here
called that) I intend
to write a natural history
of these hills. (Most plants
are primitive, some unique. My wife
says we are Adam and Eve.)
My mind's escaped old ways of seeing,
strict categories of breeding, station, class:
it roams, almost unprincipled, between
these tremendous horizons
and the new small print
used in the bibles that you've sent.
Much thanks. I wish
you could see my lake. I've made
a local version of our Oxford punt.

3

At Sunday School my dear wife reads
The Song of Solomon to a Maori chief.
He likes the *old* testament (those simple tales
of bygone kings and queens). He'll
listen for hours. His moko gleams

like blue blood on his cheeks. Once,
at a wedding feast, he ate the heart
of a living lamb – holding it up
still beating to the sun. It was
a sort of Grace – *'For what we are . . .'*
but that's perhaps difficult to understand
back in New Brighton. Suffice to say
he's *not* a violent man. He asks
why Jesus did not marry? *'The Son
of God should father sons himself.'*
A tribe of Gods! That's what he wants.
We need a priest. My poor wife does her best.

4

Our lake's one island – a sunken raft –
was once the home of cannibals.
Blood-soaked it's taken root – become
a Pavilion, a Chinese glade
of willows and bamboo. Swans
crowd there in their thousands. Some
hang themselves in their haste to breed
(long necks caught on willow forks
breasts spiked by green bamboo).
Their skeletons, so fine and white,
are delicate harps for the wind's tune.

*

At night I go down to the lake alone
haunted by the swans' cold song
(that hollow aboriginal throb). Black
swans, black eels, are all that live
in that still pond. For company
I recite to myself *The Lady of Shalott*
and see her white limbs floating past
my growing tin-roofed Camelot.
My wife's gone back. I cannot keep

her soft hands tied to this hard land.
God called her home to Camberley.
(She begs me to sell up.) I like
my lonely midnight strolls . . . eels
splashing . . . dark wings flying off.
I feel new silences. I hear Noah's doves.
I see the first hills loom above
these slow black waters fleeced in fog.

5

My wife's last letter with a pressed rose
arrived with the first snow. (How I ache
to hold her!) I've arranged my notes
in evolutionary order – according
to Lyell and Spencer. Strange
how the well-established species
show signs of regression. They 'give up'.
These acres obviously need new blood.
(Did she prick her finger? There's a stain
on the petals.) I couldn't live
without these hills, this
sense of space that goes on and on
inside my head as well as
all around me. I remember once
she said *Our pohutukawa blossoms
have the scent of salt and oranges.* That's what
this rose smells of – not Surrey
but her that summer on an Auckland beach
swimming with chestnut hair piled high
like one of Millais' women. The lake
has frozen over. Another week
and it will hold me up. I'll
skate out all alone to my island
(half-a-mile!) and count the unhatched eggs.
The swans have long gone north. Some ewes
are already lambing. In birth and death
(and love) the world goes mad.

There are no rules for our inmost feelings.
I must question Lyell and Spencer about that.

6

I'm working hard. (Six months
since I wrote you?) Lambs
to the slaughter and these endless notes!
My room is barely habitable . . .
roots, rocks, unopened bills. My drover
says that I'm being eaten up
by this 'great cannibal land'.
He's a hard worker, fresh from Yorkshire,
but a secretive and venal man.
(Some talk of crude high-country habits
and weekends at the Pa.) I've finally
got my index going. So many entries!
Where to end or begin? I've
consulted Darwin, always the best on sources,
but God still goes back further than we think.

7

'Her chestnut hair and white limbs floating . . .'
My bedroom mirror's cracked. I shave
two faces . . . or I did . . . my beard's
as thick as gorse and mad with ticks.
I've sent the first proofs off (not
happy with my quotes). The drover's left.
The front door's hanging on torn hinges.
Sheep are dying on the library steps.
The shearers are late this year. I'm lonely.
My head hurts and the blackberry patch
whimpers all night with tangled flesh.
No one comes near me. I'll leave this letter
under an ammonite. The lake keeps calling.
I'd like to lie down where the black swans nest.

A Last Note from Menton

i.m. Louis Johnson, New Zealand Poet (1924-1988)

'Displacement,' you wrote, 'is a kind
of freedom . . . Let's count ourselves lucky
we *don't* belong!' Some mention then
of how Lawrence died
in sunny Vence, with freezing legs;
while back in New Mexico his allotment bloomed
with English beans. You enjoyed a sense
of ironies on the move. They
scissored at the truth. 'In the end,'
you said, 'it's always a passing love.'

Back home, you feared we were 'digging in' . . .
that old Kiwi regressive thing
disguised as growing roots. You
fought all your life for a local voice
but knew – to misquote – that it often grew
'out of the mouths of foreign Mums.'

Again and again you mention Mansfield's
'broad light of day' – that glare
she turned away from when
it pinned her to this land. That view
has still to be faced, across
tin roofs and tidal mud. Is it
a place where only prophets thrive,
never coming down from the hills
to do the washing up? You
turned away from those cold heights
to look an exile in the eye,
living the question Katherine asked:
can one stay and keep an open heart,
discard the sackcloth, let the spirit dance?

Today I almost gave myself over
to your 'friendly enemy' Colin MaCahon.
Well, what's a little puritan thunder
when it gives you the shape
and feel of the land? But you'd
have none of him. In Mansfield's study
a print of *The Virgin as a Jug of Water*
and the Infant Jesus compared to a Lamp
made you hopping mad. 'It's
Kiwi Kindergarten stuff . . . Mum
knows best . . . the bullying voice of God!'
You slammed the door and drove to Cannes
hungry for Matisse, writing back
that 'life's too short to be preached at! Oh
these golden nudes with tits like melons
and flowers growing out of their bums!'
A kid's vernacular, poking its tongue
at stern big Daddy and know-all Mum.

We never finished our last chat
about Ashbery, that New York voice
always refusing to bore us with
'old anecdotes'. Unfair, I know,
but I had to laugh at your sudden roar
of disapproval when his language shifts
from 'the merely provisional'
to the fashionably chic. In Lambland, I guess,
we're inclined to take our egos home
bruised but intact, slapping them down
like raw steak on the page. It's as if
we *need* something 'seen-and-known,'
even 'roundly human', with which to face
the local bully on his own home-ground.

Which brings us to the question of place . . .
not always the same as feeling
we belong. 'We'll take *that*
from anywhere we can get it;
a kiss or the rim of a glass!'

You shunned a tribal embrace, that sense
of a race apart. What
mattered wasn't raising flags
but keeping love afloat. You liked
a busy harbour, boats bustling in
from London, New York, Camelot.

I think of you in a room not a landscape,
at home among 'domestic gifts' –
wife, children, friends, twin terrapins,
and that happy exile, your Australian cat
(always one up on the local mice).
A world within arm's reach . . .
the antithesis of that childhood house
with its Thirties furniture rigidly arranged
like 'a row of cold old ladies
eaten by life and work'. That place
haunted you all your life, and made
a religion for you out of hospitality:
as if your own love could erase the pain
of a prim parental parlour
reserved for guests who never arrived.
I sensed your hatred for illusions of grandeur,
your distrust of 'the new men with no qualities'
who push the vernacular aside. 'The beach
at the end of the world,' was how
you described a life-long sense
of being born marooned. What
earthed you was your love of light. (Those
huge horizons beached outside.) Each
day arrived like a guest at your door . . .

You died where you felt alive . . . in 'old Europe,'
that charnel-house of human love
where you cut through the crap of class and privilege
with such an equalising laugh. Blair
Peach died there, his skull caved in
by a bunch of *Specials* as he tried to stop
some Fascist bully-boys from playing god.

Increasingly I'm talking to the dead . . .
Jim, Renato, Stefan, yourself;
post-war émigrés and local bit-players
who belted it out, taking their bows
with more than a dash of self-conscious sweat.

Detail . . . detail . . . garlic and lemons
in a blue bowl, the moon near full,
your poems spilt like milk on the table,
the cat in the sand-box, poised like a sphinx.
I describe these things
'as they are,' as you'd find them
if you were sitting here, looking out
as Rangitoto – a tent under starlight –
with a Russian cruise-ship looming by
like that moment in Fellini's *Roma*
when the little boy looks up to find
a skyscraper silently sailing past.
Our generation's almost gone:
a handful of hermits and refugees
who loosened local speech, but rarely
shaped the language with a conscious grace.
You wrote that you 'couldn't will our history
to hide behind a settler's fence'.
What a relief! All that anxious ancestry
now left to others. Your poems adrift
like paper boats or messages in bottles,
careless of landfall, happy to be themselves.

5

Embarkations

1991 – 1996

PART ONE

'I was in an inhabited country,
but one which was as yet unknown.'

– Samuel Butler *Erewhon*

Dracula in the Auckland Hills

After so many wars and worn-out cities
I grew sick of spilt blood, of angry mobs,
mass graves, death camps, endless slaughter . . .
with my last strength I flew south to live
among these crumbling Edwardian villas,
fat abbatoirs and muddy hills. Old
Igor loves it here . . . my kauri coffin's
kept waxed and polished; my dinner-suit's
darned to the last black thread.
Both are useless now . . . one, a reminder
of a grim mortality I'm too fat to fit;
the other, of decadent nights when I danced
in crimson bordellos with naked brides,
nuzzling their creamy breasts. We still
cling to bad habits when Igor limps
at dusk along these wooden floors
to whisper . . . 'It begins!' Faint
stirrings trickle down my back.
I flap work sleeves like useless wings.
In the bedroom mirror some toothless stranger
sips his midnight milk, and grins.

*

When memories burn with former pleasures
(that sweet ache for a lost baroque)
I cool old lusts in jade-green waters
under scarlet blossoms that look like blood.
I bathe naked, letting salt and sand
scour me back to some simpler being. Even
Igor breathes deeper, strolling empty beaches
resplendent in his cloak and gloves. All
night his violin sobs across dark paddocks
like a lost child scared of the moon's huge grin
or the ocean's endless roar that shakes
the porcelain on my coffin-lid. It's
our table now, topped with vases
of 'naked ladies' and mushrooms heaped
in rimu bowls like soft white skulls.

*

Guilt . . . guilt . . . I cringe at the ancient horrors
my past brings with it. Yet I sense
the same ills in this silent bush.
Man has been here some years before me
burning roofs and bayoneting flesh. Smoke
from the chimneys of the local cannery
brings back fears I'd hoped were crushed.
So much for 'new beginnings'. I'm haunted
by the ghosts of our century steaming in
with their leather luggage, artillery, causes,
borders changing again and again . . .
Memory trembles with sad occasions,
with crowded wharfs and wayside stations
where the numberless dead wander
lost between trains . . .

We sit in the sun outside Ron the Poms
as nubile joggers go bouncing past
without so much as a downwards glance
at two old codgers, minus hair and teeth,
reading TRUTH and drinking their vodkas neat.

In Albert Park

The statue of Queen Victoria (with pout
and hooded lids) still sees
'a home away from home' . . . neat lawns,
a gravel path, English flowers,
and the one big gun – dreams of *Dear Albert* –
that continually threatens to overbalance
and topple into the town. 'Well worth
a brief visit,' the guide-book says,
while warning of muggers and 'the growing threat
of sitting unshaded in our southern sun'.

Further advice hurries over a history
dependent on imported blood,
suggesting we 'take a short-cut down
to the business district' (a photo shows
a forty-foot Santa on Farmers Store
winking like a dirty old man). For some
this park is a place apart (note
the lovers and drunks) but for most
it's an open space to be crossed
without looking back – stopping

just long enough to scoff
a Big Mac or re-set one's watch
to the scented ticking of a marigold clock.
Meanwhile, in the pause between then and now
(as preserved in the bronze folds
of a dead Queen's dress)
a bell-bird explores varieties of silence
and harbour sounds drift cautiously inland
like echoes of old arrivals and departures
scatters in the new-mown grass.

Wellington 1955

Fucking – in print – hasn't been invented
and the clitoris is a rumour . . .
no one knows where it is. In
Seatoun Zoo the last orangutan
freezes to death in an open cage
with a sack pulled over its head.
Entrails from a Hutt Valley abattoir
foul city beaches. The sea is red
with wounded Moby Dicks. Death's
rich . . . both priests and backstreet abortionists
lay down the ground-rules for a life without sin.
Up on the Terrace Ex-Nazis teach Nietzsche
while down in the harbour refugee ships
bring more walking wounded from exhausted Europe
to till fresh fields and play their violins.
(What's local has got a fist like an All-Black
and downs ten jars between five and six.)
But the scent of something more than meanness
is blowing in with the Cook Straight wind:
poets are beginning to burn their soap-box
while girls with pony-tails kick their heels
to rhythms that are more than meek. In
fugged-up coffee-bars 'the young and restless'
light black candles and plan their escape.

Home Bay

                    snugly named
with a rowing boat chained like a sleeping dog
to steps cut into clay. There's
even a wooden wharf, once built
for ferry trips but now decayed. It's
a bottom-of-the-garden bay
by-passed by surfies and marina buffs
where residents from *The Home for the Aged*
slowly descend from Hope Street
with both hands on the rail. (How
gently they undress in the shade!) There's
a resident heron, some small jade waves,
and a single thin tin shed on stilts
that seems to be stumbling out to sea.

St Kevin's Arcade – Auckland

1

St Kevin's Arcade has seen better days
but never, even in art-deco years,
a more fervent display of sale-flags. Each
stall is a small dictatorship exporting
mild porn, old bath-mats, yesterday's bread. In
the pet shop a crippled magpie croaks
obscenities to the gritty strains
of Vivaldi on a cracked LP. Near the till
a chipped china lady with borzois waves
her hat at *something* . . . 'times past'
perhaps . . . or to come? Either way
life's fun when it pretends to be cheap
and price-tags rustle like bamboo in the wind.

2

The view through mildewed café windows
could be downtown Capri . . . streets
tumbling towards a distant volcano,
the scent of jasmin, 'a sapphire sea'. OK,
so it's only the pet shop burning
broken joss-sticks, but the marble staircase
is worthy of an entrance by de Mille
while the deco wall-nudes (long boarded up)
are early Hollywood. We've stumbled upon
the ruins of that Shangri-La
our ancestors swore blind once promised
an endless life-on-the-town. In
the foyer *Junk City* spreads its beds
like a row of dreamboats blown to bits.

3

Across the road the old Egyptian *Odeon*
has swopped its towers and minarets
for a Sixties second-storey selling
Oxfam clothes and frozen fish. EL
CHEAPO RULES has been spray-painted
above a warning that TE KOOTI LIVES. Lost
youth? . . . lost loves? There's a 'haunted' air
in the deco-echoes that surround
this crumbling arcade's wooden stalls
with their island sales girls' Gauguin smiles.
Every price-tag is an act of faith,
every sale-flag a shout of praise
in a world of cough-drops and woollen knickers
that even the schoolkids refuse to pinch.

4

The magpie does his Long John Silver hop
to eat my pie's potato top
burned to a dread 'black spot'. So

much of one's life comes second-hand
it's small wonder I feel at home among
these flag-filled stalls
and deco shops. If I sit here
long enough, take communion from
this coffee cup, share a broken crust
with that unlikely 'dove', then surely
all will be revealed. Look up!
Already it begins . . . the sun
descends through domes of coloured glass;
the crippled magpie dances on clipped wings.

I go out walking . . .

not minding my own business
but giving myself up to the pleasures of the day
as they offer themselves in intimate abundance
from moment to moment along Sarsfield Street.

I wave to pale ancients in pyjamas and slippers
– wanderers from the Old Men's Home –
as they steal fiejoas from the jewelled villas
of downtown layers on fenced estates.

Then I stumble down to the beach on crumbling
civic steps that stink of rot,
emerging through bush and palm-tree alleys
'from darkness into light'.

Eagerly I strip down to embrace
the elemental as something lost,
baptizing my flesh in cool jade waves
and replacing a borrowed Walkman with

two sea-shells tuned to the lost drowned hum
of orchestras from sunken liners
or pearly porpoises making love. Then on
up a zig-zag path (where schoolboys

dive from red trees and sun-baked rocks),
stopping off at the second-hand bookshop
to buy poets from 'the barren Fifties' . . . friends
who fell into silence or an early grave

or who sailed away on the SS *Parnassus*
seeking a more romantic age. At
RAMAS FOODMART I choose huge melons
remembering (again!) those post-war years

when sandy silverbeet and bitter lemons
kept us going from birth to birth. In
The Junk Shop on the corner of Jervois Rd
I'm a child among pre-Forties kitsch.

(What once was 'home' is now bad taste . . .
black men with money-box mouths and
cheap ceramics of naked girls
who tangoed through council-house estates.)

Coming back down Hamilton Drive I notice
a noon-day moon like a dead sheep's skull
stuck on our new tin roof. (It's
'the far-away near-by'.) Inside

waiting mosquitoes scent my settled blood.

Homage to Van Der Velden
(1834-1913)

for Brian Turner

Light is seeing . . .
is love . . . is God. That's
Petrus Van Der Velden
painting the sun
and noting *these islands*
are the first to see dawn.
Van Gogh knew him (light
has no borders) and said
he had *a God-given eye.*
Certainly his subjects 'live'.
His tramps and wayfarers
have big hands and feet
that grip on solitude. They
wear their shabbiness
like a second skin. These
traits ennoble them
with nothing less
than an inner light,
a living breath. But
it's only old Van Der Velden,
Vincent's friend,
stuck in Arthurs Pass
with his pen-and-ink,
his 'huge simplicities',
his tramps and gorges,
his outmoded love
for the soul of man.

At Bland Bay – Northland

Forebears with thin-faced sheep sailing south
to 'put on meat' but lose the speech
and fleece 'that held start winter out'. Late
nineteenth-century dalesmen, yeoman stock
from border country near the Westmorland hills,
'encouraged' to leave for warmer climes
where loneliness stuck old place-names
into new ground. Beech,
elm, and mountain oak still stand
in shaded spots between puriri trees,
manuka, native scrub. The sea
and sky retain a vastness that
would come as no surprise, except
'for a light that dazzled Yorkshire eyes'
(a letter from the past) and
'pounded clay hills to dust'. All
gone now . . . all that early flesh
long underground. The lonely farms
clutching what ghosts there are close
to their hearths; the beaches
white as frozen fells. Just
these dry-stone walls left
and a few northern names . . .
their open vowels ripening in the sun.

Remembering the Fifties – Hutt Valley

As background there's this mushroom cloud
and the smell of burnt flesh. No one breathes
for fear of disturbing the Dads returning
home to scream in their war-torn sleep. In
the streets there's a glazed suburban stillness
with only the odd sad housewife weeping
behind tight hedges and trim blinds. Kids
sense an air of convalescence
but suspect that hiding 'somewhere out there'
is a madman disguised as one of the crowd.
Darkness brings relief . . . seething with old gothic dreams
the State has long discarded. Flesh
is what we most fear. It keeps
pushing through our pants and corsets
pretending to be real. Each day
totters by on new high-heels
with seams aligned and smoke-stained fingers.
The light, it has to be said, is dazzling . . .

.

Going down to the sea . . .

through acanthus and succulents
in a tumble of wooden steps
(Orpheus seeking Eurydice;
the damp anaemia of rot) then
stumbling into a light that has always,
as Grandma warned, 'dried us up' . . .

fading the photos I've used to discover
this old Edwardian bandstand where
glue-sniffers giggle
into plastic bags. The landscapes match
but these sepia ladies
with their parasols and picnic rugs

have quietly moved on . . . along
with the band, ancestral trams,
pale servant girls, and Jack-the-lads
lounging against a well-flagged seawall
while waiting for their boat-trip
to the Somme. What

remains is an orphaned feeling,
as if they'd left us here marooned.
Even their ghosts grow bored with us –
these photos whiten into abstract shapes.
The broken bandstand leans inland
like the wreck of some dismasted hulk.

At Karekari

for Kay and Karl Stead

Not another cat squawling
in the possum trap? No,
nearer now, it's that 'mad sea'
pounding a beach so hot it sent us
hopping back to Kay's
brown bread and cheese. For years
these cliffs were a weekend cave
where your kids grew as strong
as Karl's new steps (built
from iron bolts, rocks, logs,
with a raw solidity almost at odds
with his poet's post-Poundian breath). They
lead through new kauris to a balcony
overlooking 'untouched hills'. There,
tuis (fewer now) flew down
for scraps, poems
fluttered in (and out), kids
bruised new bruises crashing through
a resurgent bush that – now they've gone –
seems, suddenly, to be closing in. And
that sea . . . so much louder now . . . does it
drown out a domestic past? Almost,
but not past laughter, not
that tenderness I sense in every
pop-up book or abandoned snorkel
slowly but surely gathering dust. That
love's past on, crossing oceans. It's
an absence that hangs in the air like mist
as we brush black sand from our camembert
and 'distance looks our way' once again.

The Last Colonial

We surrounded his house at dawn (mock-
Tudor with imported battlements). The moat
his ancestors dug out by hand
had long since soured into a pond
stinking of dead sheep and DDT. We
crossed at night, expecting resistance
(following reports of him running naked
with a cutlass and scaring the deer)
but the cannons outside his gates were purely
ornamental. When we took him away
tame keas on little silver chains
wailed like peacocks on the lawn. We
levelled those rococo walls. (They
kept him from being one of ourselves.)
But his eyes stayed 'rooted to the spot'
which was strange because
we'd never thought of him as being at home
or even part of the place. He was old,
stuck in his ways, a pale
reminder of the bad old days
when harbours were thick with foreign ships,
dancing girls, and dead whales. They say
his exit is all for the best
leaving space for government flats and
plans for another Marae. (There's
even talk of a Tourist Park
with special rates for those with hard cash.)
Left to ourselves and freed of his kind
these, at last, are exciting times.

Travelling Players

I wanted nothing to do with them,
those dead relatives and parents
from another country, another age,
but they gathered round like travelling players
desperate for somewhere to stay. 'Go away,'
I yelled, 'and take your scenery with you
with its footlights, mirrors, collapsable chairs.'
Life, after all, is not a Bradford theatre
with Dad as Marvello in top-hat and cape
and Mother in bright Edwardian tights. 'But you,'
they insisted, 'are the last who lived with us,
heard our voices, touched our flesh.
After you we are only period faces
in a pile of fading junk-shop snaps!'
What could I do but renege and let them
share my life for a few more years? How
quickly they make themselves at home,
swopping their dated anecdotes and complaining
when I doze off or turn on the TV.

– Auckland

PART TWO

The Lost Child

Increasingly the past insists
it's more mysterious than what's left
(with clouds asleep on some childhood pond
and summer rooted to the spot).
But what of that child himself, the one
who roamed those former fields?
Glance back and he slips out of reach.
(Each scene has grown 'a life of its own'
ignoring the boy who gave it breath.)

Or perhaps that child is simply hiding?
Slowly counting to a hundred until
I cry out 'Coming!' and start running backwards –
as darkness thickens – to where it all began,
back beyond the first bird singing,
the first light, back beyond that.
Perhaps then he'll join me, past recalling,
leaping out and laughing
as we both become one.

A Council-House Kitchen –
Staffordshire 1946

A twelve-year-old with a toasting fork
roasts his knuckles on the kitchen grate.

Dry crusts, scraped with mutton fat,
bubble to an edible grey.

The worst storms for a decade crack
windows criss-crossed with sticky tape.

Coal's 'non-domestic' so Dad's burning slate
and back-numbers of *Lilliput*.

How quickly those prim nudes
fade away! On the wireless

plays by Eliot and Fry
remind us that our betters talk in verse.

Night after night we stare, pink-faced,
into draughty splutterings, mists, red caves,

turning our backs on 'the world outside'
and feeding our small lives to the flames.

On the Edge of the Moors – Bradford 1948

God was there, locked in a pocket-
bible with leather straps and
maps of Old Palestine – inscribed
To Joseph Whalley Bland
from the Thackley Wesleyan Sunday School . . .
a memento 1899. Dad, as a child,
singing psalms in a chapel up on Baildon Hill
doesn't fit with the father with a Passchendaele limp
who left in the slump for the Barbary Coast
to trade in whisky and cigars. Before him,
a cold wind whistled along cobblestones
and the Brontës finished their five-mile walk
climbing the stile in great-Grandad's road
to borrow books from *The Workers Educational Hall*
(returning, skirts trailing, weighed down with words,
to their graveyard rectory loud with crows). In
great-Grandad's house on the edge of the moors
I remember thinking that God still lived
stranded among kind maiden aunts
who pedalled out their Sunday hymns.
They were the ones who brought Dad home;
washed-off the stain of foreign climes;
laid-out his body in that bare front room
where I hid behind his coffin lid
and found that dusty bible thrust
under the floorboards with his school report
and some mildewed photos of French Maids.

Escape – Scarborough 1939

Mum's got on her best silk dress – blue
with pink roses – and left the washing 'to rot'
because the sun's shining and Geraldo's Band
is playing down on the Prom. I'm thrust
into fresh grey shorts and white socks
with a lick of her spit in my hair. It's
a rush keeping up with her sudden love
for the open air, for her top-of-the-bus
view of the harbour . . . but it's fun
with Mum daubed in new TABU and the men
tipping their boaters and buying me pop. When
I hide away in the herring sheds
she drifts off arm-in-arm with some toff
to sit in the shade on the castle bank. Her laugh
is as loud as the gulls that crowd
the harbour wall, or the steam-whistle blaze
of trawlers landing their catch. It's
cold though in those icy sheds. The fish-
girls wear wire mittens and clogs and
their faces are fringed with frost. Not like Mum
in white high-heels and lace gloves
with pearly powder dabbed on her cheeks
from a compact enamelled with swans. All
the way home she smiles in that glass . . .
brushing crushed leaves from her summer frock.

Scarborough 1943

Anne Brontë's loneliness chills the air
above her grave on Castle Hill. Does she
walk the battlements like Cathy calling
for her sisters' arms, her brother's
drunken kiss? Ghosts
are no more than terrible longings. I'm
fourteen and I know these things.

Down on the beach there's a dead airman.
'Is he theirs or ours?' the grown-ups ask.
Can't they see he's beyond all borders?
Don't they know how close he's come to them?
Death's everywhere. He keeps me jumping
but I'm razor-sharp . . . like those girls with cold hands
who wait on the wharf for the day's first herrings
then fillet them down to the pink.

At midnight, when the bombs go off,
I creep out from under the stairs
to watch the world in flames and to give
thin Anne bouquets of winter flowers. Desire's
icy . . . yet how sweet it is
to share her bed, to love only her,
to talk to the earth, to bring black twigs.

Painting a Childhood Primitive (circa 1943)

The happy Jack-Tar waving ripe bananas
is my newly drowned brother hurrying home
with heavenly wartime treats. And
the ghostly housewife in sky-blue pyjamas

posing against the outside loo
is Mum being a Hollywood star. (I'd guess
she's Hedy Lamarr in *White Cargo*. She's got
a rose in her hair and a far-away look.) In
the top right-hand corner I've drawn a Stuka
dive-bombing Dad's allotment where
a butterfly dries its wings. The departed
are everywhere, sadly dated;
family mostly; one schoolfriend I hated
and lovers or would-be lovers who've faded
into lives of their own. There's
no shortage of events or faces
when confronted by the garrulous dead
all crammed between the railway lines
and the new municipal tip. It's what
to leave out that's the problem . . .
the horizon of course, they can do without that,
and the yellow-brick road that begins and ends
behind every garden shed. In a last
ditch effort to cheer things up
I've painted a posh Victorian station
with a bar and lots of stained glass. There
the century can forget itself
in wreaths of gothic steam. (Even here
war-wounded walk on to the tracks!) Note
the station guard in his big black hat
with his club and three-headed dog. It must
mean *something*! What 'pops up'
can always be trusted . . . a tree . . . a pond . . .
a battered suitcase . . . boats moving off
and people waving, always that. Look,
the earth is like water beneath their feet;
the bombed streets build and rebuild themselves.

What Happened to Tonto?

A memory of Saturday morning pictures

Good Indian, man of few words,
with no known history or destination,
arriving 'in the nick of time' on
your trusty piebald (small, with no stirrups,
so that your bare feet brushed the cactus)
did you never feel a stab of envy
at *his* white charger with its jewelled leather
rearing at sunset from the rim
of the canyon? How
his guns flashed! How ladies flocked
to be in at the kill (wives bored stiff
with frontier husbands and a nagging wind
forever blowing dust on the carpet). Did
you never fancy those wives yourself
or Belle or Daisy fresh from Frisco? They
say you only lived for him. Even so
you were always my favourite, the man
with *no* mask who guarded his back
and found secret escape routes
through the forest. Did you
end up marrying that squaw who does
the rain-dance down at Union Station,
sire three kids, praise the Great White Father?
Or finally, when the last reel faded,
did you slit his kerchiefed throat and laugh,
galloping off with his horse and cash,
with his black silk mask, with Belle and Daisy?

The Station

What am I doing here, at this wayside station,
alone, wrapped in wreaths of steam,
wiping clean the carriage window
(1940s THIRD CLASS) with a childhood sleeve?
It's disturbing not knowing how I got here
or where this is leading, or whether the scene
is déjà vu or a recurring dream. It's
dark up ahead, with barriers or a crossing
and a dog barking . . . but the track behind
leads back in time to where *someone's* waving,
struggling in the distance to make themselves known.

I remember, on the way here, admiring the ruins,
and the hayfields, and people being baptized
in a stream where children caught silver minnows
but it all seems dated, a lifetime ago
or longer even. (These fittings are Edwardian
with button-seats, brass lamps, and posters
of Baden-Baden and Lake Como.) Now
there's this dim-lit provincial platform
at the end of the century, with its border posts,
as the train lurches forward and guards demand papers,
crossing my name off as they slide back the door.

Heaven

on earth of course, with a gateway of sorts
where you hang around blinded with light
but sensing a good thing
when you almost see it. Does
everyone notice the palms (mixed-in
with some childhood apple trees) or are these
simply another received idea
from the man-in-white who made wine and washed feet
as if everything he touched
had to burst into blossom? Anyway
wherever it is (or was) it's summer
and everyone's lying around in the fields
with plenty to drink and eat
in a world of their own
shared by others. Which, I suppose,
only makes sense if you're there . . . like the ladder
I remember with an orchard leaning against it,
and an angel (I swear!) climbing out of the leaves,
and the well with the sound of nothingness filling,
and the water (or was it wine?)
and the apples high-up. But you'd
have to be at one with everything
that lived and breathed under the sun
before you could *begin* to know that place
or actually reach those ripening fruits.

Greeting the Dead

Perhaps, without knowing,
I call them back? And yet
they walk through the house with such aplomb
in their Forties clothes and Panama hats
you'd think they owned the place. Their
presence could mean I've nothing left to say
to the living . . . that the young see me
much as I view these family ghosts,
sensing they populate a century of change
without identity or roots. Flags wave
with brash certainty hereabouts
while those bedding down with a few battered bags
are reminders of a transience
no one wants to admit. Like us
these ancestors are simply 'passing through'.
In their own time they shrink out of sight
to where sounds gather. (A cattle-
truck leaving. A machine-gun
starting up.) Long after
they've left there's still the faint scent
of lavender water, or someone's last cigarette.

More Poems for Jo

1 *Beach Dog*

tracking his own scent
to the sea, nose and tongue
leading him to the edge of things,
that damp sandy border where elements meet
and scents go on and on. Once there
he tries to bury himself,
digging 'down to the source'. Some dogs

go water-mad, swimming off
to the other side of the sun. This
hound's beach-bound. He won't budge.
We have to carry him back to the car,
feeding him tit-bits until he forgets
his happy death-wish. Locked indoors
he howls at high-tide and dribbles sand.

2. *Bear Begging*

A heap of blubber in a brown hair-shirt. He
hoists himself up and that hair-shirt rolls

down to his ankles. He's earthed in fat.
He's fast. He can catch like a bird. He

mouths from thin air the nuts and buns
we throw across a deep crevasse. We

hurl a sudden flurry of bread. He's not
put off. He knows just how far he can stretch.

He leans across the lip of his world
and swallows only the choicest bits.

3 *Owl Passing*

An owl in the headlamps
white in the glare. Gone

not in a flash
but with a measured thump

of muscled wings
and what sounds like breath.

There should be a sign
on the road – OWL

PASSING – and his picture
white on black. You press

my foot on the pedal . . .

You're owl-haunted!

Doing sixty there's a prickling
above our bent necks.

4 *Winter Bees*

    frost-fringed
fur stiffly chilled
they're blown indoors
to drown in milk
or mob the After-Shave

one licks the petals
printed on a rug
another fills thin leg-pads
with spilt flour. These
are desperate hours!

        Outside
the dark is closing in

PART THREE

'The universal is the local without walls.'

— Miguel Torga

At Aldeburgh

for Herbert Lomas

It's the intimacy that appeals
even here on the beach
where the sea so delicately
licks our feet, moving heaps
of pebbles back and forth

although, occasionally, you warn
it floods the path
between *Ye Olde Tea Shoppe*
and that Martello Tower
they hire out by the month.

That risk apart (and what's a storm
between a poet and his buttered scones?)
it's a landscape that seems so sure of itself
with a sense of tradition
my mind lacks. I envy you

your place here . . . at home
between engrossed extremes:
the sea, going nowhere where you'd rather be,
and those little lanes through summer fields
that lose themselves as they move inland.

A Postcard from Piccadilly

for Kevin Ireland

Strictly speaking this can't be
a New Zealand poem, it's got beggars in it,
and its streets are thronged with multitudes
'who babble a thousand divers tongues'.
(One local wag has written up
ENGLISH SPOKEN HERE on his shop.)

Last week the anti-Rushdie lot
held up our bus: kids, apeing Dad,
raged past with razored cheeks and skulls
dripping 'holy blood'. (Back East
they'd have gladly strung me up
for yelling out that God is Love.)

I was in the next street when the Harrod's bomb
blew up a florist's van. (No joke
that bitter rain of marigolds and blood!)
In the National Gallery Sheba's queen
leaves for the unknown, bathed in a light
partaking of the infinite. Outside

young Eros points his arrows at
a Porno Shop – while, beneath his feet,
kids snort 'the real thing', bedding down
in doorways all along *The Strand*. This
town's my home-away-from-home . . .
an ancestral voice that calls me back

to lay fresh flowers on paupers' graves
and prowl the dark like nutty Jack.
Alone we are born, and alone . . . the rest
you know. I'm swaying back and forth
at midnight on the Northern Line,
afloat upon a sea of souls,

sighing for those gone underground.

A Thames Tourist Boat . . .

with white lifebuoys stuck to its sides
and a Dunkirk flag. We're on board
an Edwardian gunboat or *The African Queen*
or that studio-on-water that Monet built
out of a workman's hut. We've got
a boat-for-all-seasons look. Up front
a man with a microphone helps to unroll
'the centuries preserved on either bank' . . .
that church where William Blake got spliced;
the bench where Turner outstared the sun.
(No mention of McCann's old dredger
beached like a whale with a petrified spout
or Mortlake brewery's golden drains
where kids fish the yeasty foam for sprats.)
A lonely police-launch beetles past
with something wrapped in a black plastic bag.
But that's another trip. Right now
Putney bridge floats overhead
like an ancient biplane gracefully leaving
its place in history . . . and sailing out
towards some broader element.

Sunstroke on Putney Pier

Tourist boats are Noah's Arks
with giraffes – or masts with spotted flags –
leaning into the breeze. Light screams
from cut water as dinghies froth
and bicker in mid-stream.

Eight cannibals (everything's going black)
'row . . . row . . . row' their raft
gently towards Kew. Geese,
shaped like a jet, honk past at ten decibels
and smash the Orangery to jewels.

Inside my head giant ferns uncurl
with a succulent smack of wet roots.

Eliot's 'brown god' is coming home!

All night I hear Paul Robeson singing
Aeee-a-ko . . . Aeee-a-ko . . .

His voice is throbbing like a paddle-boat.
His eyes are huge colonial moons.

The Park-Keeper as Hero

You've painted the swings bright Calder blue.
Kids swoop sky-high. You mostly stoop,
cursing the intricate floral clock
that breaks your back four times a year.
Left to yourself you'd 'plant bamboo'.
These flowers they truck-in by the week
are 'petal explosions for the tourist trade'.

The river is everywhere. Its light lassoes
the lemon and bougainvillea shoots
you're trying to coax against a southern wall.
It's there you've placed your pensioners' bench . . .
a ragged backrow left listening to the band
and applauding the same act day after day –
the sun, at Putney, doing its 'Dying Swan'
like an overworked chorus girl in scarlet tights.

Survivors

Max – TRANS GLOBAL PHYSIO –
'I gave Bush the push'
parks his live-in van where Beverley Brook
pours oil into the Thames. His dog –
Alsatian cross – marks that spot
with the compulsive vigour of one who fears
they'll soon be asked to move on. What
he doesn't know is that his master's love
embraces emergencies. Strapped to that van
are twin parachutes, a mountain bicycle,
a letter from Nixon, and a fold-up yacht.

At Zennor

Eighty years since Lawrence headed west
with his 'Hun wife' to this cottage-cave.
In London, zeppelins 'like new moons' let go
their death-seeds, turning stones to blood.
'We must build a place apart,' he wrote . . .
remembering, perhaps, the village where he'd lived
safe in his mother's arms, the surrounding farms
opening their doors to let him in. Now,
driving past Frieda's 'house of hate'
I watch waves beating on the same cold rocks
where she danced like Isadora, trailing scarfs
the locals swore were signalling German subs.
'It's Heaven here,' Lawrence lied to Murry.
'I've called it Katherine's Tower. You *must* come.'
Dressed in a pinny Lawrence waited
to kiss his handsome 'soul-mate' on the lips!
A mad house . . . with Frieda nagging him
'to earn *something*'; cursing

his 'useless influencial friends';
lecturing him on 'the mean-minded English';
begging him to sell recipes for bread.
Where was the sexual visionary she'd married?
the greatest literary genius of his age . . .
Doing embroidery by the fireside!
Copying coy pictures from womens' magazines!
And then that sudden girlish passion
for some local ploughboy who worked these hills.
God knows what happened there. And all this
with storms and soldiers roaring round the house
and Katherine seeing things, crying out 'My dead brother!'
when some major from Bodmin thundered in
calling them traitors, telling K to get dressed
as she sat on the stairs like Ophelia, clutching
violets and smoking French cigarettes.
So long ago! So many ghosts! In Padstow
they're selling souvenirs of this drab spot:
blackened bricks 'guaranteed from the original hearth'
and art-nouveau bits of a broken lamp
from happier days at the Café Royal.

Overheard in Malibu

Sir, as a visitor 'stunned' by our spaces,
desert silences, endless skies,
how *should* we populate vacancy – this
boredom brooding above the sprinklers,
these vast horizons at the end of the drive?

You note, in passing, that we build our homes
'in a plethora of imported styles' – Greek,
Roman, Elizabethan – all at odds
with our 'lack of roots', but you smile
at the burglar alarm's Mickey Mouse chimes.

And the light, you write, 'is like a glance from God'.
That's cute. We love your Gothic wit.
You Europeans are so *surrealist* . . . damn,
there's another coyote in the pool! You conclude
we're most at home when we stroll

through the cool of endless shopping malls;
that we live 'in suburbs like giant parking lots
sprawled on the edge of space . . .'
You see us as lapsed moralists
hiding behind our shades

avoiding that 'bright stare into nothingness'
that glitters above these waves
where, westward, the Pacific
(how well you put it)
'endlessly uncurls its nerveless blue'.

Near Pela – Northern Greece

There are more dead deities than tourists
on dull days with Mt Olympus
lost in smog. God after God
is stacked on the same spot;
the last, a thin Byzantine Christ
worn to a few mosaic tiles;
his eyes scuffed blind; his flattened cross
lost in the new spring grass where moths
scatter their instant wings. Far
from the forum or public baths
one senses that these ancient Gods
prefer being pensioned off. After all
most were born somewhere quiet . . .

some forgotten backwater where they wandered wild
before being hauled behind walls. At
their feet there's a scurrying;
a pooling of something;
a shimmer of Coke-cans and green lizards.

The Refugee Habit

I've got the refugee habit. Aren't I the lucky one! They say it's been
passed on. Well, whatever the circumstances – which are mixed and
changing, with the scent of wharfs and wayside stations rising above
them – just getting this far has been a miracle. When they ask me
where I come from I'm usually struck dumb. It's a symptom of my
condition . . . like the constant sound of the sea in my ageing inner-
ear. Faced with such questions I feel as though I'm about to begin the
longest poem in the world . . . the one that goes on and on long after I
do, and that stretches back beyond flags and frontiers to the Land of
Lost Recall. Mind you, looking back *can* bring things closer. I
remember an early liking for leather luggage and a childhood passion
for travel posters (preferably pre-*Titanic* but with a sprinkling of
Imperial Airways and early *P&O*). When my father died – in a desert
somewhere – the only things he left me were his broken compass and
a pair of polished but well-worn shoes. No, I tell a lie! There were
some snap-shots of my mother lying naked under a mosquito net, and
some wartime photos of young men (probably my brothers) with their
arms round a dead tank. It's been that sort of century. But, as I said,
I'm one of the lucky ones, sitting dazed by the side of the road; 'a
child of the light' (so they say) walking westwards, happy to call each
camp-fire home.

Pavements

the way, looking down, they stick in the mind
'stained with time', dog crap, blood of course,
and 'things' that live in the cracks in spite
of clumsy juggernauts and the morning crowd.

Then there's the patterning – street after street
repeating themselves with hypnotic ease
and certain abstract qualities . . .
sunlight on cobbles, shadows on stones.

But it's mostly the thought of 'the way made smooth'
by centuries of passing feet;
some sense of an earthly pilgrimage pursued
through circumstance rather than faith.

In any event, looking up, as one must
when coming to the edge of town,
I notice (with regret sometimes)
the strength with which barer elements rush in.

It's there, where pavements turn into hills,
that the lonely cult of destination . . . begins.

Exile

starts early . . . with one's first breath perhaps
or with live-in strangers called Dad and Mum.
Once in the bone though, it goes on.
Good citizens recognize the limp
you carry from place to place
bed to bed. They beg you
to be gone! Your touch
could turn their palaces into tents;
their fortresses into dust. It's said
they sense a lost part of themselves
in your vacant stare and bleeding foot. Across
the moat between you something like love
shines in their eyes as they raise their guns.

A Potential Poem for More than
Passing Strangers

Let's call it home as we turn to each other
at day's end and unpack our bags
glad to be more than passing strangers
in scenes that seem to have
chosen us . . .
                    Not bad
but going in one direction
so that, in time (and fairly soon)
the poem will get trapped in its own convention
dragged down by its 'lyric tone'.
                              Start again.
We call it home. We turn to each other . . .
Too personal. Shared egos are smug.
Try the third person, currently popular
with those who believe the poem has no speaker

other than the language itself . . .
They call it home. They turn to each other.
It's getting late. They unpack their bags . . .
Better. More mystery. An exactness of tone
from a voice that's stepped outside itself.
What's lost (and there is always leakage)
has something to do with not being involved.
I miss some sense of a living body
that someone, somewhere, has known and loved.

I'll finish this later, keeping in mind
its hints of 'a journey', imagining perhaps
(or at least) how the path
through childhood woods to a road-block culture
must have passed through many moods, many lands,
leaving no one settled, least of all this couple
who've probably suffered a century of change
but who pause, still lost, outside this poem,
refusing to be turned away.

River Landscape with Horseman and Peasants

for Michael Cronin

A world complete! Created whole by Cuyp.
Signed, I'll bet, on the seventh day.
We both gawp, being suddenly *there*
bathed by yellow light in a country lane
on the way to a burgomaster's heaven:
hills modest; towns intimate;
houses growing out of the earth –
and one lone horseman
like the man from the Pru
asking directions, passing the time of day
by the side of a summer lake. Not
a bad place to live . . . warm loaves, goats' milk,

140

all the fortresses in ruins: and this light
like warm ice, beaming benevolence,
glazing earth and air with barely a ripple.
But look, in those bushes, Cuyp's deliberate error,
the snake in the grass of this little Eden:
behind his long barrel one dark noonday figure
whitens his trigger-finger at a flock of mallards.
As we turn away the whole lake will explode
bringing death to the world,
sending that lone horseman packing . . .

from A Hermit's Notebook

after Ni Tsan

Camp Fires

The first stars . . . pale camp-fires gleaming
in a sky as black as west-coast sand. I'm
alone, as they say, but not lonely, knowing
that this dark tide slowly drifting out
(with the new moon stranded, but only for a moment,
like a yellow boat on banks of grey cloud)
is my own life quietly going nowhere,
its days deserted of bright ideas
and the last traveller home from Troy just landing
to discover his dog, long left to itself,
turning its back on a god descending
to dig for crabs and casually lift its leg.

The Silence

A mountain hut, an old stone bridge,
skies torn apart by cliffs, and a stream
babbling in praise of the picturesque . . .
Like most good things I stumbled upon them

taking the wrong path, thinking it led to the sea
then, suddenly, looming up, saw these ruins
quarried out of the living rock.
The silence here must have drawn me inland . . .
the way it goes further and further back
beyond bee-stir, spider-scratchings,
the creaking skins of ripening plums.

At Home

I've fed the crows their morning milk.
(They're moving closer to my hut
each day.) A stray cat
passed in the dark. (It drained
the hedgehog's water-dish
before drifting on to better things
or the hope of them.) Last night
even the stars came closer,
feeding on my midnight gaze. By day
ants that battle for my fallen crumbs
are just as numerous . . . while, camped indoors,
fat moths chew holes in my public robes
and build their homes in damp forgotten furs.

The Lady of the House

Among the axe-heads and stone phalluses
buried in this old earth floor,
I've discovered one gold ear-ring
and hung it, by a hair, on my door.
A thing so fine that, nightly I lie alone
and listen to its tinkling in thin air . . .
sweet music left here by the lady of the house.

Visitors

The dead again! Old family visitors.
Keepers, perhaps, of some 'shared soul'.
Why this persistence, merely to wander
my borrowed house at a loss for words?
Do I keep them here with a mind engrossed
by unfinished business? Am I coming home
to those dark borders where the dead and living
stumble into each other's arms? How
beautiful they are! How life haunts them!
Nightly they warm themselves at my stove.

Smoke in the Valleys

Smoke in the valleys . . .
more War-Lords gathering;
ships from the other side of the sun;
sudden migrations; whole cities dying;
armies of preachers babbling in tongues.
None of us, at peace in these mountains,
are above these things or beyond their touch
(the snowline bleeds with smoke and dust).
There's a restlessness at the heart of matter,
a thin bleak nomad who rules within . . .
We fear him even here, his anger,
his grim refusal to sit still.

Embarkations

Paintings by Claude Lorraine

Someone's leaving: in every scene
someone's stepping into the sea.

History is at their backs – the dream
of a Golden Age in pastoral ruins.

It's a journey they'll make just once
so they travel light – their going noticed

only by the beasts of the field
whose look, never changing,

moves us as much as this setting out
beyond human love – or into it,

whichever is waiting. They go alone
along the sun's path, not looking back

but aching to be in that far country
that is nowhere and everywhere – the true home

whose radiance shines on their limbs and faces.